The Twelve Chosen Disciples

Jesus said to them:

"I will make you fishers of men"

Ian Fleck

Foreword by: Dr Chris Wright

The Twelve Chosen Disciples
Lessons from their Lives

Paperback: ISBN: 978-1-62020-193-0
eBook: ISBN: 978-1-62020-194-7

Printed by Bethel Solutions

Ambassador International
Emerald House
427 Wade Hampton Blvd
Greenville, SC 29609, USA
www.ambassador-international.com

Ambassador Books and Media
The Mount
2 Woodstock Link
Belfast, BT6 8DD, Northern Ireland, UK
www.ambassadormedia.co.uk

This book is dedicated to

Sandra and the family

who have supported and encouraged

me in the work of the Lord over the years

This is a tremendously useful book that will have a place on many a minister's bookshelf. From Andrew through to Judas, Ian Fleck's survey is detailed but accessible and never dry. This is a timely book, coming at a time when many in the church are speaking of the need for discipleship, yet, all too often, little or nothing is ever said of the first disciples. This book opens up their lives to us.

Rev. Dr. Paul Bailie
Chief Executive, Mission Africa (Working in Nigeria, Burkina Faso, Chad and Kenya)

Ian Fleck has successfully delved into a rather neglected area. He has applied his wealth of theological experience to bring together all biblical data on the twelve disciples and spiced up with relevant historical facts. The value of this sizeable book will last long especially in Gospel and Discipleship studies. A must read for every Bible student.

Rev. Dr. Effiong A. Udoeyop
Provost, Peter Achimugu College of Theology, Ankpa, Kogi State, Nigeria

Inspired by material concerning the Twelve disciples which he has assembled from the Four Gospels, and in interaction with other Scripture texts and some ancient traditions, Ian Fleck in this series of meditations has succeeded in deriving, from the lives of Jesus' chosen followers, challenging, inspirational and practical lessons for readers to apply in discipleship of Christ today.

Rev. Dr. Gordon Campbell
Professor of New Testament, Union Theological College, Belfast.

Contents

Foreword

It is rather surprising that there are very few books like this one (that I know of). When you think that the word 'disciple' occurs more than 260 times in the Gospels and Acts (whereas the word 'Christian' occurs only 3 times in the New Testament), when you recall how 'the disciples' are there on every page of the Gospels, and when you remember that we are told the names of all twelve of Jesus core group of disciples four times over (but how few of us could recite them all from memory) – it really is surprising that we very seldom stop to think about each of them as individuals and ask what we can learn from their stories.

Of course, some of them scarcely have any 'stories' that we know for certain. Others are clearly prominent in the New Testament itself. Peter, James and John – the names roll off the tongue simply because Jesus took those three with him on significant occasions – were clearly an inner circle about whom we know a lot. But since Jesus made a point of stressing to the whole group that 'greatness' was not a matter of primacy and status, we must not assume that the other ones (apart from Judas Iscariot) were any less significant in their apostleship and ministry in the spread of the gospel.

In this engaging book, Ian Fleck helps us see as much as we can of each of The Twelve as a unique individual. He helpfully collates all that the Bible tells us in the Gospels and Acts (and some epistles) about them. Along the way he draws out helpful reflections and lessons that we can learn as modern day disciples from the lives, questions, failures and faithfulness of the original disciples of our Lord. We see Him through their eyes, and we see them through His. This provides a much-needed balance to the tendency in evangelical circles to focus almost entirely on the Apostle Paul – who described himself as 'the least of the apostles' - to the neglect of those whom Jesus called and commissioned in His earthly lifetime. It also helps balance the tendency to prioritize the epistles over the gospels.

Then the author goes on to draw on other traditional materials, from the early Church Fathers and historians, to fill out as much as is known about their lives and travels in the years after Pentecost. Of course, the author does not suggest that we can have the same confidence in the historical facts behind those sources as we place on the New Testament records, but assuming that at least some of those long-standing traditions of ancient churches rest on historical roots, we are treated to a fascinating picture of how that tiny company of Galileans – fishermen, a tax-collector, a former terrorist, and others – eventually moved out to all points of the compass in the known world, in fulfilment of the great mission mandate to make disciples of all nations.

We are called not just to put our faith in Jesus for the sake of securing our eternal salvation, but to be followers of Jesus here and now. In that challenge and calling, the lives of the first disciples, in all their humanity, provide an inspiring example. This book puts us in the midst of that small company and helps us to get to know them better, and with them, to follow their Lord and ours more closely.

Christopher J. H. Wright
International Ministries Director, Langham Partnership

Preface

Many Christians are unable to give the names, or many details, of Jesus' twelve disciples and yet we can learn many lessons from their lives. Each of them had his own personality but Jesus was able to change and use them in the service of the Kingdom of God.

We have Simon Peter who was the spokesman for the disciples, but frequently said the wrong thing at important moments. He was constantly asking questions and was not afraid to argue with Jesus. He was one of the chosen inner three, whom Jesus asked to be with Him on many special occasions. On the other hand, very little was written or known about Thaddaeus and yet we can learn from both of them.

It is important to remember that the apostles were human beings like ourselves. Unlike us, they had personal face-to-face knowledge of Jesus Christ, our Saviour, and they probably saw many more remarkable miracles than we know about. Jesus chose twelve men to be His close and constant companions to be with Him at all times and in all places.

However, we can use the example of the apostles to inspire and teach us. They had faults like we do. They were a mixed bunch of men, each with their own gifts and struggles. God calls all sorts of people, and we cannot forget that Jesus was selecting men for a leadership role in the early church. He had to choose some and reject others from among a sizeable number.

The selection of the Twelve from a larger group of disciples, who had gradually gathered around Him, was an important landmark in the gospel history. At the beginning of His ministry Jesus laboured single-handed, His miraculous deeds were confined for the most part, to a small geographical area and His teaching was the plain simple gospel message.

But by the time the Twelve were chosen, the work of the gospel had grown to such an extent as to require organisation and the allocation of the work; and the teaching of Jesus was beginning to become deeper and more detailed.

We must not forget the apostles were ordinary men. Most of us can easily see some aspect of our own character in their lives, their struggles and frequent blunders, shortcomings and longing to be everything Christ wanted them to be. It gives us great hope to see how wonderfully God used people such as these.

Each disciple was unique, but each had a special place in carrying out God's work. Even Judas would have made a great contribution had he not been attracted by greed and motivated to betray Jesus Christ for thirty pieces of silver. His life also shows that not everyone who claims to be a Christian is a genuine and true member of the family of God.

It is encouraging to us to see how Jesus Christ chose men who were, for the most part, selfish and on at least one occasion were arguing over who was the greatest, but through the influence of Jesus Christ on their lives were transformed into loyal and faithful disciples. These life stories of the disciples demonstrate that Jesus can use us in spite of our weaknesses and He has the power to enable us to become people of God.

Regardless of what happened to them as they disappeared off the pages of the New Testament, we know for certain their ministries changed the course of history. They were transformed into dynamic witnesses and laid the foundation of the church.

How does one express an adequate word of appreciation to those who were so kind in their support and assistance in bringing this book to its present state, without whom this study on the twelve disciples could not have been completed. As the manuscript was being prepared I shared it chapter by chapter with a number of friends. First of all, my wife Sandra, and Mr Dennis Davis, who spent many hours reading and re-reading each chapter. I am profoundly grateful for the invaluable advice and help they gave. My special thanks also to the Rev. Eddie Kirk and the Rev. Knox Jones for their comments and advice given as they read each chapter.

I am also most grateful to the Rev. Dr. Chris Wright, who has taken the time out of his busy schedule to read the manuscript and write the Foreword. I also thank Rev. Dr. Paul Bailie, Rev. Dr. Effiong A. Udoeyop, and Rev. Dr. Gordon Campbell for their kind comments of recommendation.

I trust you will be challenged and blessed as you read this book.

Ian Fleck

May 2016

INTRODUCTION

Ask a group of churchgoers for the names of our Lord's twelve disciples and it is doubtful if they could repeat more than eight or nine. They will be able to give the names of Peter, James and John, but will struggle to remember the names of James the Less, Bartholomew, Simon the Zealot or Thaddaeus. Some may even wrongly suggest the names of Mark, Luke, Paul or Timothy. However, no small group of people in human history has made such an impact on the world as this group.

Jesus spent the first thirty years of His life virtually unknown, working as a carpenter in the village of Nazareth in Palestine. One day He went to the river Jordan where John the Baptist had been baptising his followers. Jesus was also baptised by John and the Holy Spirit descended on Him in bodily form like a dove. A voice came from heaven, *"You are my Son, whom I love; with you I am well pleased"* (Luke 3:22). Then He was led by the Spirit to the desert where, for forty days, He was tempted by Satan.

After this, Jesus returned to Galilee where He taught in the synagogues and the people praised Him. Then he went to Nazareth, where He was brought up, and continued to preach in the synagogues where *"all spoke well of him and were amazed at the gracious words that came from his lips"* (Luke 4:22).

Jesus calls His disciples to Salvation

When Jesus began His public ministry, He did not have anyone with Him. One day, He was walking near the Jordan River where John the Baptist was ministering. Andrew, John and some others were there as they were already disciples of John the Baptist. But when they heard John the Baptist single out Jesus and say, *"Look, the Lamb of God, who takes away the sin of the world"* they left John and followed Jesus (John 1:29).

As time went on, many people followed Jesus. A true disciple is one who is committed to following Jesus and recognises Jesus as the Saviour of the world. Jesus asked His disciples, *"Who do you say that I am?"* Simon Peter answered, *"You are the Christ, the Son of the living God."* Jesus affirmed Peter's faith saying, *"Blessed are you, Simon son of Jonah, for this was not revealed to you by man, but by my Father who is in heaven"* (Matthew 16:15-17).

The disciples recognised Jesus as the 'Lamb of God' and Messiah. Scripture states that, *"Everyone who believes that Jesus is the Christ is born of God ..."* (1 John 5:1). Peter believed in Christ as the Son of the living God and Jesus called him blessed for his faith and confession.

Throughout Jesus' ministry, He taught about salvation, and even spoke of certain individuals being saved. For example, Jesus said Zacchaeus was saved, *"Today salvation has come to this house"* (Luke 19:9), He also said to the paralytic, *"Take heart, son; your sins are forgiven"* (Matthew 9:2). To the sinful woman He said, *"Your sins are forgiven"* (Luke 7:48). These incidents do not make reference to "following Jesus as a disciple" but to faith and repentance. Jesus said, *"I tell you the truth, he who believes has everlasting life"* (John 6:47).

On one occasion Jesus called the crowd to Him with His disciples, and said to them, *"If anyone would come after me, he must deny himself, and take up his cross, and follow me"* (Mark 8:34). After Jesus performed miracles and challenged the crowd, we are told from that time many of His disciples turned back, and walked no more with Him. Then Jesus said to the Twelve, *"You do not want to leave too, do you?"*

In response Simon Peter answered, *"Lord, to whom shall we go? You have the words of eternal life. We believe and know that you are the Holy One of God"* (John 6:67-69). Here we see that the faith of Peter was common to the Twelve (he said "we believe"). The further context of this passage shows that Judas was the exception to this.

It shows how every disciple is called first to salvation before being called to service. At that stage, the disciples did not leave fishing as their full-time jobs. That is why we read about them fishing and mending nets. They continued as fishermen until Jesus called them to full-time ministry.

Jesus calls the Twelve

We read how one day Jesus went out into the hills to pray, and spent the night praying to God. *"When morning came, he called his disciples to him and chose twelve of them, whom he also designated apostles"* (Luke 6:12-13). Jesus chose twelve men from a larger gathering of believers to form a special group to be with Him.

These men were not of perfect character, each one of them had faults and failings. Peter called down curses on himself and swore, denying knowing Jesus. Thomas was a man who expressed his doubts about the resurrection of Jesus. Matthew was a tax collector and collaborator with the Roman authorities. James and

John wanted to call down fire on their enemies. Judas Iscariot was a deceitful and scheming person who eventually betrayed Jesus to the authorities. None of them held a high position in society and none belonged to the Pharisee or the Sadducee party.

The twelve disciples that Jesus chose would have had average schooling in the local synagogue. The Sanhedrin considered Peter and John to be *"unschooled, ordinary men"* (Acts 4:13). They were not old men, but youths, probably in their 20s. Perhaps John was in his late teens, and Peter near 30. We know Peter was married (Matthew 8:14). The Bible suggests the other apostles also had wives (1 Corinthians 9:5). They were all Jews.

In the Gospels, the term "disciple" is almost always used to refer specifically to the Twelve. The term "disciple" was also used to refer to other disciples who were not numbered among the Twelve. There are many passages that indicate that there was a larger group of disciples than just the Twelve. There were at least seventy-two men in this group (Luke 10:1). When the eleven apostles sought to replace Judas they proposed two men that were apparently part of this larger group of disciples (Acts 1:21-26).

To the Jews who had believed Him, Jesus said, *"If you hold to my teaching, you are really my disciples"* (John 8:31) and in another reference we read, *"The Pharisees heard that Jesus was gaining and baptising more disciples than John, although in fact it was not Jesus who baptised, but his disciples"* (John 4:1-2).

Jesus spent almost three years with the Twelve, teaching them about Himself and explaining to them the truths of God's Word. During that time, Jesus performed many amazing miracles, and lived a perfect and righteous life before them. The New Testament records some of the things Jesus said and miracles He carried out – healing various diseases, restoring sight to the blind, raising the dead, calming the storm and multiplying food to feed crowds of people. We would not have known about these things if they had not been witnessed by His disciples and written down.

The Lord chose 'twelve' apostles

The number twelve in the Jewish culture was something special - signifying perfection. Therefore, in order that Jesus should have the correct or perfect number of disciples, He chose twelve.

God's chosen people in the Old Testament were divided into twelve tribes. The twelve tribes of Israel came from the twelve sons of Israel. "Israel" is the name that God gave Jacob (Genesis 32:28). Jesus said there would be twelve thrones for judging the twelve tribes of Israel. *"I tell you the truth, at the renewal of all things, when the Son of Man sits on his glorious throne, you who have followed me will also sit on twelve thrones, judging the twelve tribes of Israel"* (Matthew 19:28).

The Holy City, the New Jerusalem, *"had a great, high wall with twelve gates, and with twelve angels at the gates"* (Revelation 21:12). We are told that there will be twelve pearl gates in heaven. *"The twelve gates were twelve pearls, each gate made with a single pearl"* (Revelation 21:21). The apostles themselves considered the number twelve to be significant, because Luke describes how, after Jesus' ascension, the apostles chose Matthias to fill the vacancy caused by the death of Judas (Acts 1:23-26).

Jesus personally selected twelve from a larger group of disciples after a night of prayer. Jesus' knowledge of the Twelve was comprehensive and despite being aware that Judas would betray Him, Jesus did not withhold from him any blessing or privilege (John 6:70; 13:20-27).

Jesus said, *"You did not choose me, but I chose you to go and bear fruit – fruit that will last*" (John 15:16). Jesus initially called these men "to be with him" – to be his companions and friends. Later He trained them and showed, by example, how they could go out and preach the Good News of the Gospel.

Jesus called the Twelve for a specific purpose

Jesus chose His closest followers after much prayer and consideration. He needed people He could trust to continue His work and take the Gospel to every nation when He returned to heaven.

Jesus called the twelve men for a special purpose. "*He appointed twelve ..... that they might be with him and that he might send them out to preach and to have authority to drive out demons*" (Mark 3:14-15). He also "*gave them authority to cure every kind of disease and sickness*" (Matthew 10:1).

The word 'disciple' refers to 'someone who follows another person.' While Jesus was on earth, the Twelve were called disciples and became learners and followers. They were taught and trained by Jesus as they followed Him. After Jesus' resurrection and ascension they were referred to as the twelve apostles and had been given a particular commission. The word apostle means, 'one who is sent out.'

Sometimes there are very few details in the Bible of what the apostles did, but they faithfully ministered and carried out their commission of "*go into the world and preach the gospel.*"

The apostle John wrote, "*Jesus did many other miraculous signs in the presence of his disciples, which are not recorded in this book. But these are written that you may believe that Jesus is the Christ, the Son of God, and that by believing you may have life in his name*"

(John 20:30-31). If the apostles did not record everything Jesus said and the miracles He did, then it is unlikely they would want to record the details of their own lives.

The Twelve spread the Gospel message

It is noteworthy that these men had a personal encounter with Christ as their Saviour before they went out as His messengers. It is a sad fact that there are those who want to be in the ministry, and to be preachers of the gospel, and yet they themselves have not had an experience of Christ in their own lives.

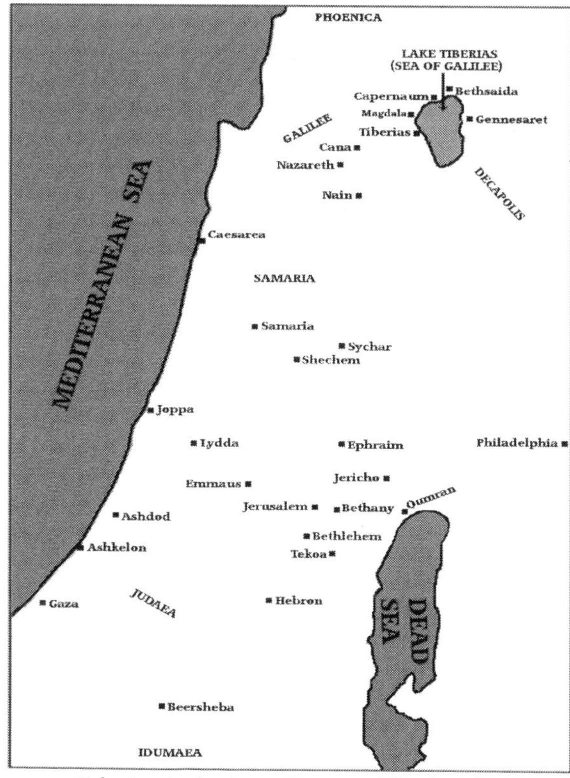

Palestine in the days of Jesus and His disciples

We are not told what qualifications Jesus used when selecting the Twelve from among the large number of disciples, apart from the fact He had known them for some time. We do know what qualifications were required for the replacement of Judas. The replacement for Judas had to be a person who had been with Jesus and the other disciples since the days of John the Baptist. He would have witnessed the teaching and miracles of Jesus on this earth and also witnessed His resurrection and ascension into heaven (Acts 1:21-26).

A great responsibility was placed upon the Twelve as they laid the structural foundation of the Church. They took the Gospel to the Jews (Acts 2:36-41); to the Samaritans (half Jews) (Acts 8:14-17) and to the Gentiles in Cornelius' household (Acts 10:30-48) and in Antioch (Acts 11:20-23). Apostolic approval was given for this work as the gospel spread around the then known world.

The New Testament tells of the fate of only two of the apostles: Judas, who betrayed Jesus and had hanged himself, and James the son of Zebedee, who was executed by Herod about AD 44 (Acts 12:2).

What happened at Pentecost caused a dramatic change in the lives of the apostles. They were never the same after it. Filled with the Holy Spirit, they were transformed from a group of discouraged and frightened men into a band of brave and courageous evangelists.

The indications from the Bible are that, for some years, the Twelve (the Eleven plus Matthias) remained in Jerusalem. Tradition says that they then decided on a strategy of world evangelism and divided up the world to determine who would go where, so all could hear about Jesus. Each apostle travelled his separate way and went to places such as Pontus, Galatia, Cappadocia, Italy, Asia, Scythia, and to the Thracians who were bordered by the Scythians to the north, the Celts and the Illyrians to the west. They also went to India, Parthia, and to the Medes who established an empire that stretched from Aran (modern-day Republic of Azerbaijan) to Central Asia and Afghanistan. Today's population of the western part of the Iranian Plateau (including many Persian-speakers, Kurds and Azeris) consider themselves to be descended from the ancient Medes. The apostles preached the Gospel in Mesopotamia, Syria, Persia, Edessa, India, Turkey, Greece, Britain, Scotland, Carthage in North Africa, Asia Minor, Ethiopia and Southern Arabia.

The Twelve were not the kind of men you might have expected Jesus to send forth on His mission to reach the world. There was nothing special or spectacular about them. They were just ordinary men, but with the teaching and training of Jesus they established the Christian church. He gave them the most amazing commission: *"Go into all the world and preach the gospel."* They called the entire world, including the mighty Roman Empire, to repentance and faith in the risen Christ and, within three centuries, the Christian faith was the official faith of the empire. The apostles suffered greatly for their faith and in most cases met violent deaths on account of their bold witness.

Non-Biblical sources about the Twelve

The history of the apostles starts in the books of the Bible. However, there were other books and documents written in the first and second century AD that were not included in the canon of Scripture.

We must remember that until the sixties of the first century AD the need for written Gospels did not appear to be needed as the disciples and other eye-witnesses were alive to tell the events. But the apostles were not going to live on earth forever and it then became obvious that the message needed to be written down to be preserved.

About the year AD 200 Irenaeus quoted from 21 books that would end up as part of the New Testament. About AD 230 Origen of Alexandria may have been using the same 27 books as in the modern New Testament, though there were still disputes over the canonicity of about six of them. The first known list of 27 books we have, appeared in a letter to the churches at Easter in AD 367, written by Athanasius, bishop of Alexandria. Shortly afterwards Jerome and Augustine defined the canon by listing the same 27 books.

The earliest Christian writers outside the New Testament are known as the Apostolic Fathers, writing between AD 80 and 180. These include, Clement of Rome, Ignatius of Antioch, Polycarp of Smyrna, The Didache, Shepherd of Hermas, Barnabas, Justin Martyr, Papias, bishop of Hierapolis and Irenaeus, bishop of Lyon,

We also have the works of Josephus who was born in Jerusalem in AD 37/38 and became a historian. He wrote '*The Jewish War*' which recounts the Jewish revolt against Roman occupation (66-70), also '*Antiquities of the Jews*' which recounts the history of the world from a Jewish perspective for a Roman audience. These works provide valuable information of the first century Judaism and religious backgrounds of the New Testament and Christianity.

The 'Shepherd of Hermas,' was known to the early Church Fathers and was a Christian literary work of the 2nd century, considered a valuable book by many Christians.

The 'Revelation of Peter,' was a piece of literature believed to have been written around the middle of the second century AD. This work should not be confused with the letters of the apostle Peter we have in the canon of Scripture.

The 'Epistle of Barnabas,' was a Greek work containing twenty-one chapters, preserved complete in the 4th century *Codex Sinaiticus*. It is traditionally attributed to the Barnabas who is mentioned in the Acts of the Apostles, though some credited it to another apostolic father of the same name.

The author of the 'Acts of Paul' is unknown and is believed to have been written out of respect of the apostle Paul and uses oral traditions of Paul's missionary work.

The 'Teachings of the Apostles,' (commonly called the *Didache)* was a brief early Christian treatise, dated by most scholars to the late first or early 2nd century.

A great deal of written material must have been lost in the destruction of Jerusalem in AD 70 and still more during the years of persecution that ended in AD 313, when Constantine the Great played an influential role in the proclamation of the Edit of Milan, which decreed tolerance for Christianity in the Roman Empire.

Eusebius (c. AD 260-339), bishop of Caesarea, (the famous city of Palestine constructed by Herod the Great on the Mediterranean shore), was the first to undertake the task of tracing the rise of Christianity during the crucial first three centuries, from Christ to Constantine. Since no other ancient author tried to cover the same period, Eusebius is our main source for earliest Christianity and his Church History is the basis on which later historians received much of their information.

What happened to Jesus' apostles later in life? Where did John spend the rest of his life? Did Paul survive his trial before Nero? How did the New Testament canon develop? Why and how were the early Christians persecuted? These questions and many more involve an era not covered by the New Testament and could not easily be answered were it not for Eusebius.

Eusebius wrote of those who had the courage to face emperors and challenge heretics; of bishops and elders who guided the church through dreadful afflictions and of writers whose influential statements conformed to the Christian faith as established by the early Church. These details would, in many cases, have been lost had Eusebius not reported them word for word. Eusebius' writings showed how many attacks against the Christians turned into victory in the course of the Church's first three centuries.

The 'Ecclesiastical History' written by Eusebius gives information about many sources and traditions that in other respects would have been lost many centuries ago. He was a careful historian who took care to reference his sources. He had at his disposal the library at Caesarea, which Origen had built up after he had been forced to leave Alexandria and took up residence in Palestine. Pamphilus, a devoted follower of Origen, had added many volumes to the library. He was the friend and teacher of Eusebius, who composed the biography of Pamphilus in three volumes. Eusebius was a man of deep humility and of great authority in the Church of his day. He was anxious to keep to the rule of faith that had come down from the apostles. The soundness of his doctrine concerning the Trinity and the Incarnation is shown in the many extracts from his writings.

Eusebius collected and organized material covering the history of the Church from the well-stocked library in Caesarea, as well as by visiting the Christian library at Jerusalem, founded in the previous century by Bishop Alexander. Eusebius' work contains ten books dealing with the life of Christ and the rise of Christendom from the ascension of Christ in AD 33 up to the reign of Diocletian.

Eusebius was able to quote from St Clement of Rome (AD 30-97), a disciple of Peter and Paul. Clement is known for his epistle to the church in Corinth (c. AD 96), in which he asserts the apostolic authority of the bishops/presbyters as rulers of the church. Clement wrote to the troubled congregation in Corinth, where certain "presbyters" or "bishops" had been deposed. Clement called for repentance and reinstatement of those who had been deposed.

Eusebius was also able to quote from Papias (AD 60-135), bishop of Hierapolis (modern Pamukkale in Turkey), and author of the '*Exposition of the Sayings of the Lord*.' Papias was probably born about AD 60, so that it is possible he may have seen and heard the aged apostle John who lived until around AD 100, and other disciples who survived the destruction of Jerusalem. His '*Interpretations of the Sayings of the Lord*,' a commentary in five books, would have been a major work in the explanation of the sayings of Jesus, some of which are recorded in the Gospels of Matthew and Luke. However, the book has not survived and is known only through fragments quoted by later writers such as Irenaeus and Eusebius.

Eusebius also quoted from Irenaeus (c. AD 120-202), bishop of Lyons, in what is now France. Irenaeus experienced the terrible treatment of the Martyrs of Lyons and Vienne in AD 177, when the Christians were persecuted during the reign of Marcus Aurelius (AD 161-180). Irenaeus composed various letters to oppose those in Rome who were rejecting the sound teaching of the church. Fragments of other letters of Irenaeus were quoted by Eusebius.

The writings of Tertullian (c. AD 145-221) were also consulted by Eusebius. Tertullian lived in the ancient city of Carthage in what is now Tunisia and was the first Christian writer to write in Latin. He wrote a great number of works. It is not known how many he wrote and not all of his works were ever completed.

Information from the writings of Clement of Alexandria (c. AD 153-217) was also used by Eusebius. He was an early Greek theologian and head of the catechetical school of Alexandria. The writings of St. Hippolytus of Rome (c. AD 170-236) were also a valuable resource for Eusebius. Hippolytus, a Greek, was a pupil of Irenaeus, who was a disciple of Polycarp, and Polycarp was a disciple of John, the beloved disciple of Jesus. Polycarp became the head of the school of theology and a bishop in Rome.

Although we are limited in the information from the New Testament about some of the twelve disciples, we can supplement that information from these scholars who were able to gather valuable information during their life time.

Lessons from the lives of the Disciples

To write about the lives of the twelve disciples, poses difficulties as in some cases, there is very little written about them. The disciples did not write about themselves, but were fully committed to their Master and on spreading the Good News that everlasting life was to be found through a personal commitment to Him.

To study the lives of the twelve chosen disciples is to get to know the men who were closest to Christ during His earthly life. To be made aware of the fact that they were ordinary people is an encouragement to us.

They were the first to follow Jesus, and we are also called to follow Him. It is wonderful to know that the same Jesus, who taught and blessed those first disciples, can do likewise for us today.

Their lives and their writings show us what they believed. Without a doubt they were all totally convinced of Jesus' deity to the end. Their conclusion, even unto death, was that Jesus was God and we can experience salvation and have everlasting life through faith in Him.

ANDREW
THE FIRST DISCIPLE

Andrew was born in Bethsaida (John 1:44), a village on the shore of the Sea of Galilee. Later, he moved with his brother Simon to a house in Capernaum (Mark 1:29). Andrew and Simon were sons of a man named John (John 1:42; 21:15-17). By profession, Andrew was a fisherman with his brother Simon on the Sea of Galilee. They worked with James and John and their father Zebedee, in his thriving fishing business (Luke 5:10).

Andrew is mentioned in Matthew, Mark and Luke in the list of disciples but it is in the Gospel of John that we find the most information about him. On several occasions, Andrew was called "Simon's brother," suggesting that people would know Simon but not Andrew.

The first mention we have of Andrew is in the company of John the Baptist. John the Baptist often reminded people that he was not the Messiah himself, but the one who was preparing the way for the Messiah. He told them that he baptised with water, but the One who would come would baptise them with the Holy Spirit (Luke 3:16).

John tells us that one day, as Jesus passed by, John the Baptist pointed to Him and said, *"Look, the Lamb of God, who takes away the sin of the world*" (John 1:29). The next day, John the Baptist was with two of his disciples, Andrew and an unnamed disciple, generally believed to be John, the author of the Gospel of John. Again, John the Baptist said, "*Look, the Lamb of God*" (John 1:36). Because Andrew and John heard what John the Baptist said about Jesus, they left him and followed Jesus.

When Jesus saw them He asked what they wanted. Perhaps because the question was unexpected, they did not know what to say and could only reply, "*Teacher, where are you staying.*" Jesus answered, "*Come and see.*" The word "see" is meaningful. The Greek word used is not '*blepo*' which means come and physically see with the bodily eyes. The Greek word used is '*eidon*' which is not physical sight but spiritual insight. This is the word used when Jesus said to Nathanael, "*I saw you while you were still under the fig-tree*" (John 1:48). 'Do you see' can mean 'sight.' 'Do you see' can also mean 'insight, discernment and perception.' Jesus was saying, 'Come and see what you are really looking for,' or 'Come and see who I am, and what I am.'

Jesus, Andrew and John spent the remainder of the day together. It would be interesting if we had some record of what they talked about, but it is obvious that, whatever it was, Andrew was convinced Jesus was the Messiah. Andrew had spent the day with Jesus and something happened during that time he had been in the presence of Jesus. Andrew was transformed and became a follower of Jesus Christ.

How Andrew was led to meet Jesus is a valuable lesson for every believer. It is by exalting Christ, not the church, not the sacraments, not the preacher, that hearts are moved and sinners turn to God.

The people who have done most in every part of the world for the cause of Christ are those who, like John the Baptist, have proclaimed, *"Look, the Lamb of God who takes away the sin of the world"* (John 1:29). They have not said, look at me the preacher, look at our beautiful church, look at the sacraments, but "*Look, the Lamb of God.*"

Christ was the great sacrifice for sin. There is no other one; there is no other way for the sinner to be saved. He was the true sacrificial Lamb. Christ came into this world to be our Saviour. He came to do that which man could never do for himself; He came to "take away sin." He "took" the punishment for our sins upon Himself.

John the Baptist proclaimed this good news to Andrew, which led to him following Jesus and being convinced that Jesus was the Messiah and Saviour of the world. Here, we see the good that can be done to others by testifying about Jesus Christ.

Andrew brought his brother Simon to Jesus

John 1:40-42

After Andrew's encounter with Jesus, his immediate reaction was to find his brother Simon Peter and tell him, *"We have found the Messiah"* (John 1:41). Perhaps Andrew's most memorable contribution to the work of God was when he brought his brother, Simon, to the Lord.

The Bible says that Andrew "brought" Simon to Jesus (John 1:42). Some believe that this word "brought" indicates that Andrew had to overcome some resistance on Simon's part. Nevertheless, Andrew convinced Simon to come to Jesus. The reason Andrew led his brother to Him was because he was convinced that Jesus was "the Christ," the Anointed One, the Messiah.

When Simon was introduced to Jesus by Andrew, Jesus said, *"You are Simon son of John, you will be called Cephas"* (which, when translated, is Peter) (John 1:42). Cephas in Aramaic and Peter in Greek mean a rock or a stone. Christ knows who we are and who we will become. He intended to change Simon, and that is what He wants for each and every one of us.

At the very first meeting, Andrew would hear Jesus indicate that Simon Peter would become chief among his disciples. Andrew is the one responsible for introducing the great apostle, Simon Peter, to Jesus.

Who can tell what might have happened to Simon if Andrew had kept the good news to himself and not witnessed to his brother! Are Christians guilty of this today? A great change took place in Simon's life and, because of this and through his life and witness, his influence has reached every generation to the present day.

We are not all called to be preachers or great apostles like Simon Peter; however, we can serve Christ as his brother Andrew did. We can search for the truth and introduce our loved ones and others to Jesus. As a result we may see lives changed. We are called to become "*Fishers of men.*"

In John's gospel, it is significant that Andrew was called directly by Jesus, while Peter was brought by Andrew to Jesus. It often happens that an ordinary person can be instrumental in witnessing to someone who will become a Christian, and who will later do great work for God.

How great a witness it would be if all men and women, who have had a personal experience with Jesus Christ, would speak to their friends and neighbours and invite them to meet Jesus as Andrew did. Many, humanly speaking, who would not attend a church and listen to a sermon, may listen to a word from a friend. They may invite them to "*Come and see*" (John 1:46b) and be surprised with the results.

Andrew brought a boy to Jesus

Matthew 14:13-21; Mark 6:30-44; Luke 9:10-17; John 6:1-15

Andrew was with Jesus and the other disciples when a great crowd followed them to the far shore of the Sea of Galilee. Jesus began to teach the people and to heal the sick. When pressed to dismiss the crowd as it was getting late in the evening, Jesus told His disciples to feed the people. He asked the disciples, "*Where shall we buy bread for these people to eat*?" Philip made a quick calculation and decided that they did not have enough money to buy the bread that would be needed (John 6:5-7).

Andrew went among the crowd to find out what was available in the way of food. He reappeared with a young boy who had only five barley loaves and a couple of fish. (Mark 6:38). The 'barley loaves' pointed to his poverty, for the wheat bread would be reserved for the upper classes of society. His willingness to hand over what little he had to the Lord, showed the commitment of this lad. The devotion of one or two can prove to be a blessing to many.

This lad had no idea that he would fit into Christ's plan, but Jesus knew. This is the second instance of Andrew introducing someone to Jesus and is the only miracle, of all the miracles that Jesus performed, that is recorded in all four Gospels. This was a meagre lunch but in Jesus' hands it fed a multitude. Jesus can multiply your ability and great things can happen when you yield what you have to Him.

Andrew brought a little boy into the presence of Jesus and Jesus was able to use his five loaves of bread and two fish to perform a miracle. Out of such a large crowd, this little unnamed boy had the opportunity to come close to the Lord. How did it happen? Andrew must have asked him to bring his lunch to Jesus.

This tells us something about Andrew. He had a deep trust in his Lord and awareness that Jesus was Master, even over the laws of nature. Philip dismissed the possibility of feeding the crowd, but Andrew realised that as long as the Lord was near, there was a solution. Just as the Lord could provide fish to weary fishermen who had toiled all night and caught nothing, then He could supply the food to feed this crowd (Luke 5:1-7).

Jesus took the boy's lunch and lifting His eyes to heaven gave thanks to God for it. Though the amount of food seemed so small, the Master miraculously multiplied it sufficiently to satisfy the need of 5,000 men plus women and children. We should follow Andrew's example and enjoy what we have in gratitude and generosity. Nothing is too little to be given for Him to use.

Many years ago a young boy attended a special evangelistic service in Scotland and he gave his life to Jesus Christ. Some were disappointed that he was the only result of the special services. Little did they realise that thousands would be won to Christ, and the continent of Africa would be opened up for the gospel through him in the years to follow. His name was David Livingstone. Many people can testify that they became involved in a church, or had contact with Christian friends, simply because someone showed interest in them.

Andrew and his brother Peter had very different methods of witnessing for Christ. We are told that Peter preached at Pentecost and 3,000 people were added to the church (Acts 2:14-41). We have no reference in the Gospels to any occasion when Andrew preached to a great crowd with many being saved as a result. But remember it was Andrew who brought Peter to Christ. Therefore, the fruit from Peter's ministry is ultimately also the fruit of Andrew's faithful individual witness. God often works that way.

On one occasion a teenage boy went to Boston from Northfield,

Massachusetts. He felt all alone in the big city, but an uncle gave him a job as a shoe salesman. A Sunday school teacher by the name of Edward Kimball took a great interest in this teenager. He went to the shoe shop on April 21, 1855 and witnessed to him with the result he gave his life to Christ. That young man was D.L. Moody, who immediately began sharing his faith with others, including his own family. Kimball felt very unworthy to witness to Moody and later said he had never seen anyone whose mind was as spiritually dark as that of D.L. Moody.

D.L. Moody was mightily used by God as an evangelist both in America and England. He had a passion for saving souls and determined never to let a day pass without telling someone the gospel of Jesus Christ. Among his converts were people like C.T. Studd, who was converted to Christ during a Moody-Sankey campaign in England in 1877, and who faithfully served His Saviour in China, India, and Africa.

Later, Moody founded the Moody Bible Institute, where thousands of missionaries, evangelists and other Christian workers have been trained and sent throughout the world. All of that began when one man called Edward Kimball took the courage to witness in faltering words to a young rebellious youth about his Saviour.

Andrew demonstrated great faith in our Lord when he brought the boy with his small lunch to feed 5,000 people. We need 'Andrews' today to bring boys and girls to Christ. We live in a society when second and third generations of children know nothing of Jesus. Teenagers are using alcohol and drugs, oblivious of what Christ has done for them on the cross.

Some of the disciples were focusing upon the difficulty of getting food for such a large crowd. However, in the midst of all this difficulty, we see the commitment of Andrew and the result.

Andrew brought Greeks to see Jesus
(John 12:20-33)

On the day following Jesus' entry into Jerusalem, He entered the temple area and drove out those who were buying and selling there (Matthew 21:12; Mark 11:15; Luke 19:45). As this area was open to everyone, it was called the 'Court of the Gentiles.' It may be that the Greeks (Gentiles), who wanted to see Jesus, had witnessed what Jesus had just done.

These Greeks first approached Philip with the request, "*Sir, we would like to see Jesus.*" We are told "*They came to Philip, who was from Bethsaida*" (John 12:21). Perhaps they came to Philip because he had a Greek name and Greek connections, though John does not say why they came to him.

They came to Philip but he must have been unsure of what to do in that situation. Perhaps he thought salvation was only for the Jews. Had he gone to Peter, James, or John, he might have been told that Jesus would not be interested in talking to the Greeks, as Jesus was sent to the Jews first. However, Philip spoke to Andrew and together they went to tell Jesus about it.

Andrew had previously brought a boy to Jesus when looking for food to feed more than 5,000 people. On this occasion, Andrew did not hesitate but simply told Jesus about the Greeks' request, trusting Him to deal with the situation, as He did before with the boy. He understood that Jesus would be interested in anyone who wanted to meet Him. Jesus had already said, "*whoever comes to me I will never drive away*" (John 6:37).

We are not told specifically if Jesus met these Greeks but look at the response Jesus gave to Andrew when the request was made. We are told that Jesus answered by predicting His own death. He said, "*The hour is come, that the Son of Man should be glorified*" (John 12:23). Jesus must suffer and die in order that men and women might be saved. Apart from His death, the life of Jesus could not have saved one sinner. Jesus told the disciples that He must pass through death and resurrection.

Jesus recognised in this request from these Gentiles, the beginning of a great harvest from among the nations; an evidence of what would take place in the whole Gentile world in the years to follow.

Jesus was anticipating His death at Calvary and the result of this sacrifice. He shared a message on bearing fruit, which would be possible through His work as He said, "*Unless an ear of wheat falls to the ground and dies, it remains only a single seed. But if it dies, it produces many seeds*" (John 12:24).

If people in our neighbourhood are interested in spiritual matters like the Greeks in our text, we must follow the example of Andrew and Philip and lovingly point them to Jesus.

Andrew's Final Years

The last mention of Andrew in the New Testament comes when the disciples and others met in the upper room at Jerusalem. They were praying and waiting for the promised Holy Spirit (Acts 1:13-14). On the day of Pentecost, the Holy Spirit came upon them and Andrew would have been present to witness and take part in this experience. After this, he played his part in the remarkable expansion of the church, although we are told nothing of his apostolic labours. The Bible does not record in the book of Acts what happened to Andrew after Pentecost, but from other sources we are given information about his ministry and death.

Tradition says he took the gospel north. Eusebius, the ancient church historian, says he went as far as Scythia, the area around the Black Sea in southern Russia. Because he ministered in Scythia as far as the Caspian Sea, Andrew was named patron saint of Russia by the Russian Orthodox Church.

He finally reached Byzantium (present day Istanbul) and there ordained Bishop Stachys. From Byzantium he continued to Greece. Hence Andrew also became known as the patron saint of Greece. He travelled to Thrace and Macedonia down through the Corinthian Gulf to Patras. It was in Patras that Andrew was to preach the Gospel of Christ for the last time.

Through his preaching and the miracles of healing he performed in the name of Jesus, many people were converted to Christianity. Among those healed was Maximilla, the wife of the Roman Proconsul, Aegeates. Seeing this miracle of healing, Stratoklis, the brother of the Proconsul, also became a Christian, and Andrew consecrated and enthroned him as the first Bishop of Patras.

Aegeates, the governor, heard about this and wanted no part of the new religion. He came to Patras to put an end to the Christian movement there. To do this, he enforced a legal requirement that everyone worship the Roman gods by making sacrifices to them. Andrew refused and went to Aegeates and tried to persuade him to leave the false gods of the Romans and turn to the one true God, Jesus Christ. Aegeates had Andrew arrested and put in prison.

Andrew was crucified in Patras, at the place where the Basilica now stands, on an X-shaped (saltire) cross, which is still known as the Saint Andrew's cross. They did not nail him there but sought to prolong his agony by binding him so that he would die a slow lingering death of hunger, thirst and exposure. Tradition has it that he suffered there for three days preaching to all who passed by during his conscious hours. The crucifixion was carried out during the reign of Nero, and Andrew died on 30 November, AD 60 or, according to others, in AD 69.

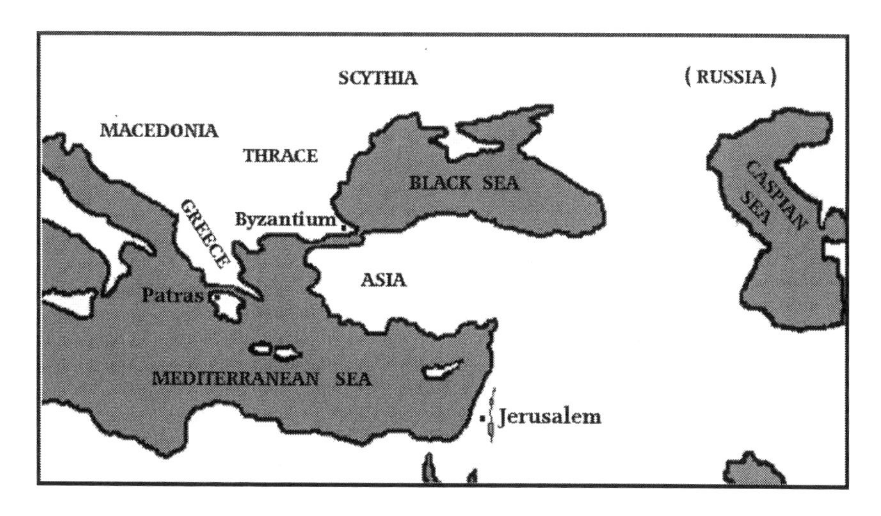

Map of places Andrew visited

His body was lovingly removed from the cross by Bishop Stratoklis and Maximilla, and buried with all the honour befitting the Apostle. After his burial, large numbers of Christians made their way to Patras to pay respect at the grave of Andrew. In the month of March, AD 357, the Emperor Constantine (son of Constantine the Great) ordered that the body of Saint Andrew be removed and placed in the altar of the Church of the Holy Apostles in Byzantium (Istanbul). The head of Andrew remained in Patras.

A few bones reputed to be those of Andrew were found in Constantinople and transported to Scotland by a Christian named St. Regulus, in the fourth or fifth century. They were buried at a place which was later called "St. Andrews".

Today the apostle is the patron saint of Scotland, and St. Andrew's Cross is the official symbol of that country with his cross being displayed on the flag of Scotland and also on the union flag of the United Kingdom. *St. Andrew's Day is celebrated annually in Scotland on 30 November.* In 2006, the Scottish Parliament designated St. Andrew's Day as an official bank holiday, and Scotland has a university named after him. It is also a national holiday in Romania.

In 1462, Pope Pius II transferred the head of Andrew to Italy and placed it in the Church of Saint Peter for safekeeping after the Turks had swept through Byzantium (Istanbul). It remained there in Italy until 1964 when Pope Paul VI had it returned to the Episcopal See of the Greek Orthodox Church in Patras, Greece, where Andrew was martyred.

The relics of Andrew are kept in the New Church of St. Andrew in Patras, in a special tomb, and are reverenced every November 30 in a special ceremony. The cross of St. Andrew upon which he was martyred, is also kept in the New Church of St. Andrew, near the Saint's relics.

Final Comment

Andrew was an average man, but he accomplished much, therefore his character is an important study. Andrew had a keen interest in other people. He was a man of discernment, love, zeal and obedience.

One of the commendable things about Andrew was his willingness to take second place. He is usually referred to as "Simon Peter's brother." Peter, James and John were always mentioned before Andrew. From the order in which the twelve disciples occur in the various lists of the Twelve given in the Gospels, Andrew is mentioned fourth - therefore in the opinion of the authors was regarded higher than the eight but not quite as high as the three.

There is no suggestion that Andrew had any feelings of jealousy or resentment that he could do as well as any of them or perhaps better. Surely it was because of Andrew that Peter came to know Jesus Christ in the first place. Andrew was a humble man who had no ambitions for himself to take a place of importance, his only desire was to see God glorified and people come to know Him. Andrew was not among the group of disciples who were arguing among themselves as to who was the greatest and have first place.

Andrew was always available to bring others to Jesus – he brought his brother Simon to Jesus; he brought the boy with his lunch to Jesus to feed a hungry crowd of people; he brought the Greeks to Jesus who made the request to Philip that they wanted to see Jesus. Andrew knew anyone who wanted to meet Jesus was a person that Jesus would want to meet.

Andrew had a passion for introducing people to Christ. When he found out about the Messiah, his first action was to find his brother and share the good news. His faithfulness produced results for the kingdom. It could be said that it was because of Andrew's faithfulness in witnessing to Peter that led to three thousand hearing the gospel and accepting Christ. Andrew's ministry was different from his brother's but both their ministries were very valuable.

We don't know what happened concerning the Greeks about whom Andrew went to see Jesus. It could have been the opening up of another great ministry opportunity. Sometimes we won't know what our faithfulness did for the kingdom, but we must be faithful.

Andrew went quietly about his job, winning people one-by-one. The 'Andrews' of our churches seldom preach from influential pulpits. They teach small Sunday school classes, Bible study groups, or small youth fellowships. The church needs its 'Peters' who are up front in proclaiming Christ, but it cannot get along without the quiet 'Andrews,' ministering faithfully behind the scenes.

May we have the passion that Andrew had and the desire for the people around us to know who Jesus is. May we realize that the love of God is for everyone and that our faithfulness in sharing about God's love can produce results we never imagined.

JAMES
THE SON OF ZEBEDEE

There are three men named James in the Bible. All three had much in common, so it is easy to confuse them – each one had a brother and all three were martyred in Jerusalem.

a) James, the son of Zebedee. By comparing Matthew 27:56 with Mark 15:40; 16:1, we can determine that his mother's name was Salome.

b) James, the son of Alphaeus – also known as "James, the Less" (Matthew 10:3). His mother's name was Mary (Mark 15:40).

c) Perhaps the best known of the three was James, our Lord's brother, who was not one of the original disciples. His mother's name was obviously Mary (Matthew 13:55). During Jesus' lifetime, His family severely criticized Jesus for what He was doing and saying, and did not believe Him to be the Messiah. Mark gives an account of how Jesus' family had been so concerned about Him, that they "*went to take charge of Him, for they said, 'He is out of his mind*'" (Mark 3:21).

It is suggested that this problem caused a rift between Jesus' brothers and sisters and His mother, because at the cross Jesus asked the apostle John to care for His mother. However, we thank God that a wonderful and mysterious change took place in James' life. After Jesus' resurrection, 1 Corinthians 15:7 tells us, "Then he appeared to James."

Obviously, James came to realise that Jesus was the Messiah and had been converted after the resurrection. It is amazing how the one who initially opposed Jesus came to be a "pillar" in the church and the first bishop of Jerusalem. After the martyrdom of the apostle James, this James, the brother of Jesus, became the Pastor (elder) of the Church at Jerusalem (Acts 12:17; 15:13; 21:18; Galatians 1:19). Although not one of the Twelve, James, the brother of Jesus, like Paul, had the authority of an apostle and was the author of the epistle of James. He is also called James the Greater to distinguish him from James, son of Alphaeus, who is also known as James the Less.

Jesus calls James to follow Him

We read that Jesus called Simon and Andrew when they were "*casting a net into the lake*" (Mark 1:16), and James and John when they were "*preparing their nets*" (Mark 1: 19). Jesus did not call His disciples from the elite of society but ordinary men. God often calls 'ordinary' people to do a special work – Moses was keeping sheep, Gideon was threshing wheat, Elisha was ploughing, David was a shepherd boy and these first disciples were fishermen.

When Jesus called James, the son of Zebedee, he left a thriving fishing business behind, with the security that it gave, in order to follow Him. James was the older brother of John, which is why he is always mentioned before John. As the eldest, he had family rights that were well known traditions in Israel. His father, Zebedee, was a wealthy and influential man. This could explain how James' family knew the High Priest and how John was able to gain access to the courtyard while Peter had to wait outside before Jesus' trial (John 18:15-16).

Jesus must have considered James to have great potential and ability since he had been selected as one of the inner circle. These three disciples (Peter, James and John) witnessed many things that the other nine did not witness, including raising Jairus' daughter from the dead (Mark 5:37) and Jesus' transfiguration (Matthew 17:1). In spite of this privileged position, we know comparatively little about James. He is always mentioned in scripture with his brother John; the only time he is referred to by himself is when his martyrdom had been mentioned in Acts 12:2.

Some historians believe that as it is recorded, Salome, the mother of James, witnessed the crucifixion (Mark 15:40), and is likely to be the unnamed fourth woman mentioned as "his mother's sister" in John 19:25. She stood at a distance with the mother of Jesus, Mary the wife of Cleophas, and Mary Magdalene. This deduction would make Salome the aunt of Jesus, and her sons His first-cousins. If this is correct, then it would help to explain why the mother of James and John asked for them to sit at Jesus' side in heaven.

James witnessed Jairus' daughter being healed

(Mark 5:37; Luke 8:51)

Jairus, a ruler of the synagogue, came to Jesus begging Him to go and heal his sick daughter. Jesus immediately started to go with him, but He was delayed on the road by a woman. This woman, who had been with many doctors over the years, came up behind Jesus and touched the edge of His cloak, believing that by such an action she would be healed. Luke, the doctor, wrote that this woman had spent all her money on doctors' fees, yet none of them could heal her. Luke obviously recognised the seriousness of her case and the desperate situation she found herself in.

So this poor sick woman, pressed her way through the crowd because she had faith that Jesus could do what no other person could do, heal her. However, she was reluctant to come out in the open to meet Jesus the way Jairus had come for His help. Nevertheless, she displayed remarkable faith in believing that if only she touched the hem of His cloak, she would be healed.

Jesus knew immediately what had happened and stopped to ask "*Who touched me?*" When no one admitted touching Jesus, Peter spoke up to tell Him that the crowd was pressing against him, so obviously someone had touched Him. Jesus knew that power had gone out from Him and someone had touched Him for a reason, not just a crowd crushing against Him.

We are told that when the woman saw that what she had done became known, she "*came trembling and fell at His feet.*" In the presence of everyone, she told them what had happened and how she had been healed. It was a wonderful testimony to the power of Jesus Christ in her life. Here we see how immediate and instantaneous was the healing this woman received. The healing that she had earnestly sought for twelve years happened in a moment. In like manner, when a sinner comes to the Saviour for cleansing from sin, that person receives immediate relief and forgiveness.

However, this woman had not been allowed to slip away unnoticed. Jesus enquired who touched Him. He did this so that she would confess publicly what had happened to her. In like manner the one, who has received cleansing and forgiveness from sin, should not be ashamed to confess Christ before others as to what He has done for their soul.

All this activity delayed Jesus going to Jairus' house, which must have been exceedingly frustrating for Jairus, who was eager to take Jesus to his daughter. Almost immediately, someone came to tell Jairus that his daughter was dead and not to bother the teacher any more. They implied that if Jesus had gone sooner there would have been some hope that He could have helped her, but it was now too late.

This was devastating news for Jairus who had urgently and sincerely come to Jesus to heal his sick daughter, but now it would appear to be all in vain. On hearing the news about the girl, Jesus turned to Jairus and said, "*Don't be afraid; just believe, and she will be healed.*" Jairus was about to see a mighty miracle that Jesus had not only power over sickness but also over death.

When they arrived at the house, Jesus allowed the girl's parents and His three disciples, Peter, James and John, to enter the room with Him. Jesus also told those who were outside the house wailing to stop, as the girl was not dead. They laughed at Him for they knew without a doubt that the child was dead.

Jesus took the little girl by the hand and said, "*My child, get up.*" At once she stood up and Jesus told her parents to give her something to eat. What an experience that must have been for the parents to see their little girl stand up! We are told that her parents were "astonished." Not only did this girl come back to life, but had also been healed of her sickness, getting out of bed and starting to eat.

Let us see in this miracle, proof of what Jesus can do for those who are dead in trespasses and sins; He will raise them up in newness of life. Jesus gives us hope of eternal life, because He has risen from the dead - alive forever. One day He will raise those who believe in Him to live with him forever. We have a great hope and a great God.

Not only did the parents of the girl witness this miracle but James, John and Peter also had been witnesses. When they had arrived at the home there was weeping and wailing over the death of a young girl, but the weeping changed to rejoicing when she had been restored to perfect health.

James and John wanted to call down fire on their Enemies
(Luke 9:51-56)

After the amazing experience of Peter, James and John going up a mountain with Jesus where He had been transfigured before them and where He talked to Moses and Elijah, the Bible records that Jesus realized His time to be crucified was at hand and set his face resolutely towards Jerusalem.

To get to Jerusalem, which was quite a distance south of Galilee, the group decided to go the shortest route through the Samaritan mountains. They had taken this route in the past, when Jesus met the Samaritan woman at Jacob's Well. Most Jews would not risk going through Samaria, and the same could be said for the Samaritans, as they were reluctant to go through Israel. Their hatred for each other had been going on for centuries. Only Luke's Gospel records this incident.

The Samaritans were a mixed race of Jews from the Northern Kingdom. When Israel had been conquered by the Assyrians, the most prominent and influential people in the tribes were taken into captivity. The land was then resettled with these Assyrians and foreigners who had been loyal to the Assyrian king (2 Kings 17:24-41). Poor Israelites who remained in the land intermarried with these inhabitants and were called Samaritans. Hatred developed over the years between these Samaritans and the pure Jews so it is no surprise that this village would reject Jesus as He travelled towards Jerusalem. The Samaritans not only hated the Jews, they hated the worship that took place in Jerusalem, because in reality they took the worship of Jehovah and mixed it with other pagan religions.

Jesus was heading for Jerusalem to celebrate the Passover; however, the Samaritans believed that such feasts and ceremonies should be observed on Mount Gerizim. This hostility between the Samaritans and Jews was clearly displayed when Jesus met the woman at the well and asked her for a drink of water. Her reply was, "' *You are a Jew and I am a Samaritan woman. How can you ask me for a drink?' (For the Jews do not associate with Samaritans)*" (John 4:9).

Religious intolerance is very unpleasant when one group of religious people look with suspicion upon those of another. What damage has been done to the cause of Christ when denominations, churches and Christians quarrel and disagree over petty matters!

History reveals that thousands have been burned, shot, hanged, drowned and persecuted, in the name of God; and those who have carried out such acts have actually believed that they were doing God a service. May we never be tempted directly or indirectly to discredit, malign or persecute another person under the pretence of doing that which is for the good of the kingdom of God.

As Jesus and His disciples travelled in Samaria, He sent some messengers ahead to reserve a place to stay and to have something to eat. No doubt the disciples were not entirely in favour of this request due to the hatred between the Jews and the Samaritans. However, it is unlikely that they were expecting the reply they received. The Samaritans refused Jesus' request. If He was going to Jerusalem with His disciples to worship, He would have to go another way and not through their territory.

This triggered a quick response from James and John – to call down fire in judgement upon them as Elijah had done. This was a reference to Elijah calling down fire on the fifty men that King Ahaziah had sent to arrest him. Elijah said to the captain of the men, "*If I am a man of God, may fire come down from heaven and consume you and your fifty men*" (2 Kings 1:10). As a result, fire came down and consumed them all.

When Jesus sent out His disciples two by two to preach, He told them if a town or village would not receive them, they were to shake the dust off their feet when they left. He said, "*It will be more bearable for Sodom and Gomorrah on the day of judgment than for that town*" (Matthew 10:15). Perhaps James and John considered that if Sodom and Gomorrah had been destroyed by fire from heaven then Jesus would consent to their request for similar treatment on this Samaritan town. James and John's response shows just how far they were from sharing Jesus' commitment to the way of the cross!

James and John ask for a place of honour

(Matthew 20:20-28; Mark 10:35-45)

Mark tells us James and John came to Jesus and said to Him, "*Teacher, we want you to do for us whatever we ask of you.*" So Jesus asked what they wanted and they replied, "*Let us sit at your right and the other at your left in your glory.*"

Here they displayed evidence of arrogance, pride and self-importance; far removed from what Jesus had just been teaching them about humility. Jesus used this opportunity for further teaching on humility; not to behave as many leaders in the world do, and not to rule as many humans rule. Rather than modelling themselves after the example of Jesus, the disciples were making the mistake of following the example of the Roman rulers who loved position and authority.

These men believed that, according to Jesus' promise, one day He would be seated on the throne of His glory and that each of the twelve disciples would also be seated on their thrones. Earlier Peter had asked Jesus what he and the other apostles, who had left everything to follow Him, would receive in return. Jesus answered that when the "*Son of Man sits on his glorious throne, you will also sit on twelve thrones, judging the twelve tribes of Israel*" (Matthew 19:28).

Perhaps these disciples were requesting to sit near their Master even though there was no evidence that such a thing was soon to happen. When James and John made their request, it was just after Jesus had told them how His own life was going to end, in suffering, crucifixion and the resurrection. When the brothers heard this on the road to Jerusalem, they had been shocked by it.

After hearing about the agonies that were only days away for their Master, the disciples were still selfishly grasping for power. James and John put in their request before Peter or the others could do so.

In spite of being with Jesus for a number of years and listening to His teaching, James and John held to the belief that Christ's kingdom on earth was soon to take place. These men pictured Jesus as sitting on His throne with many officials around Him and with them occupying the highest honour by His side.

Obviously a selfish, sinful motive and ambition was being revealed here. They desired to have the two most honourable places assigned not to Peter, Philip, Andrew or any of the other disciples but to themselves, James and John. They did not seem to remember that true greatness does not consist in being someone of importance in this life, rather in seeking to serve the Lord. People of this world may laugh at us, mock and ridicule us or even persecute us, but our names are written in heaven where we will receive the 'well done, good and faithful servant.'

Who made this Request?

It is not clear who was behind this request. Was it James and John themselves or was it their mother? When Matthew records this incident he says, "*Then the mother of Zebedee's sons came to Jesus with her sons and, kneeling down, asked a favour of him*" (Matthew 20:20-21).

The mother could have been asking this favour for her sons on her own behalf, or James and John could have asked their mother to make the request on their behalf. Notice that Jesus directs His answer, not to the mother who asked the question, but to both James and John. This would be in agreement with Mark's account of the incident.

Since James and John's mother was Salome, the sister of Mary the mother of Jesus, she was an aunt of Jesus. Was this aunt now using her influence to make the request that her sons, who were cousins of Jesus, be given this honour (Matthew 27:56; Mark 15:40; John 19:25)?

Just before this incident, Jesus had been emphasizing that in His kingdom greatness is measured by humility (Matthew 18:1-4). In spite of all His teaching about humility and service, we have the mother of James and John making the request for her sons to be placed in the two highest positions in the kingdom.

The cost of those two positions

How does the loving Lord Jesus answer this request? "'*You don't know what you are asking,*' Jesus said, '*Can you drink the cup I drink or be baptised with the baptism I am baptised with?*'" (Mark

10:38). James and John were full of confidence that they could, and would be able to endure anything that might come their way. They were confident that they would be able to drink of their Master's cup and be baptised with their Master's baptism.

The fundamental mistake they were making was to ignore the other events that would take place in Jerusalem. Was the Lord not emphasising the coming events; the betrayal, the mockery, the spitting, the flogging, and the death? James and John were dismissing the cross. All they had in their minds was His resurrection and their seats alongside Him in glory, but it was solely because of these events that Jesus would reach His journey's end. Jesus reminds them of something they seemed to have forgotten, that a request for glory is a request for suffering – it is the way of the cross that leads to heaven and home.

Jesus said, "You don't know what you are asking. Do you know the price of those two seats? The price is a 'cup' that has to be drunk and a fearful baptism." That was the way Jesus must go, by the cup He had to drink and the baptism with which He had to be baptised.

What He was saying to them was that He was going up to Jerusalem to suffer death on the cross. What a cup of hatred He would have to drink! What a baptism of affliction He would have to endure! He was going to Jerusalem to face judicial murder by the most terrible torture. That was Jesus' route to His throne; it had to be via Golgotha. So the Lord underlines this by way of two vivid metaphors – the cup and the baptism.

James and John with their mother, had asked for thrones, but Jesus made it clear that there can be no glory apart from suffering.

James was arrested and killed, and John became an exile on the Isle of Patmos, a prisoner of Rome. Indeed, they did drink of the cup and share in the baptism of suffering that their Lord had experienced.

A lesson for all the disciples

Hearing this conversation, the other ten disciples became very displeased with James and John, but Jesus seized the moment to teach all of them a lesson.

Jesus called them together and said, "*Whoever wants to be first must be slave of all.*" The Greek word used for "slave" is *doulos*, which means, 'a servant, a slave, or one devoted to another to the disregard of one's own interest.' The person who is a servant of Jesus will set aside his or her own interests and seek to live for Jesus. Jesus said, "*For even the Son of Man did not come to be served, but to serve, and to give his life as a ransom for many*" (Mark 10:45).

Jesus had set the example of what it means to serve when, as the disciples walked along the road to Capernaum, they discussed which of them was the greatest. Jesus had challenged them to be like a little child (Mark 9:33-37).

Perhaps we should daily ask ourselves, are we looking out for our own interests or His? Do we want to be served or to serve? Which choice will we make?

Could it be that the ten other disciples had been upset at the insensitivity of the two asking for this position in the Kingdom? Perhaps they did not have the right motives either.

This issue comes up even on the night Christ had been betrayed - His last night with the disciples. Every one of the disciples wanted a place of honour. They were indignant that James and John had asked because Jesus might have given those places to His cousins. As a result the ten remaining disciples would have to accept other positions in the Kingdom. This thought caused them to react in the way they did.

The ten disciples complained because James and John wanted important positions in heaven. That is human nature. Some people will do whatever it takes to get what they desire. This is the way of the world, greed, envy and ambition - there is no such thing as an ambitious man who is truly satisfied. Christ understood this. He understood the desire for greatness as the world sees it.

Jesus said, *"to sit at my right or left is not for me to grant. These places belong to those for whom they have been prepared"* (v.40). Jesus taught the disciples that no one will be granted glory in the kingdom of God by organising a pressure group. It does not work like that in the kingdom of God. Jesus said, *"To sit at my right or left is not for me to grant."* It is not in Jesus' will or power to grant honours in His kingdom through partiality and patronage.

To be with Christ you must come as you are and seek His cleansing and forgiveness of sins. The Psalmist cried out to God, *"Search me, O God, and know my heart; test me and know my anxious thoughts. See if there be any offensive way in me, and lead me in the way everlasting"* (Psalm 139:23-24).

James in Gethsemane

(Matthew 26:36-46; Mark 14:32-42)

We are familiar with the Garden of Gethsemane because of what happened there and the betrayal of the LORD into the hands of the *"chief priests and elders of the people"* (Matthew 26:47). Before His betrayal that night in Gethsemane, we are reminded of the nature of Jesus› agony when He prayed, *"Father, if you are willing, take this cup from me; yet not my will, but yours be done"* (Luke 22:42). Scripture records that immediately *"an angel from Heaven appeared to him and strengthened him"* (22:43), in response to His petition.

Shortly before Christ's prayer in Gethsemane, He and His disciples had observed the Passover Supper, which we now commemorate as the "Lord's Supper" (1Corinthians 11:20). They came to Gethsemane, where the LORD told the eleven, *"Sit here, while I go over there and pray"* (Matthew 26:36). Taking with Him Peter, James and John from the remaining disciples, Jesus *"withdrew about a stone's throw beyond them"* (Luke 22:41). Jesus said to them, *"My soul is over-whelmed with sorrow to the point of death. Stay here and keep watch with me"* (Matthew 26:38). These were the Lord's closest earthly friends of which He asked their support in preparation for His death on the Cross. They would overhear Jesus say, *"Abba, Father, everything is possible for you. Take this cup from me. Yet not what I will, but what you will"* (Mark 14:36).

It was not that His will did not match the Father's will, because the Lord Jesus certainly was one with the Father. *"That all of them may be one, Father, just as you are in me and I am in you"* (John 17:21). Jesus just wanted to emphasize that it was the Father's will that mattered, not His own. Dr. Luke wrote: *"And being in anguish, he prayed more earnestly, and his sweat was like drops of blood falling to the ground"* (Luke 22:44).

Peter, James and John had just returned from an amazing experience on the Mount of Transfiguration when Jesus was transfigured before them and *"His face shone like the sun, and his clothes became as white as the light"* (Matthew 17:2). They were so amazed and excited when they saw Moses and Elijah talking to Jesus that they wanted to build three shelters, one for Jesus and one each for Moses and Elijah. However, now in the Garden of Gethsemane they lost interest and fell asleep when Jesus went alone to pray.

Jesus' agony in the Garden of Gethsemane was not caused by the prospect of coming face to face with physical death or the thought of being betrayed by Judas, a friend and disciple; nor His rejection by Israel's religious leaders and their condemnation of Him; nor the scattering of His eleven disciples, when they would forsake Him and flee upon His arrest, all these things Jesus had known before He was 'sorrowful and troubled' in the garden. Indeed, He had already experienced the rejection and persecution of the religious leaders and the rejection by His home town of Nazareth. He had even taught the disciples to 'rejoice and be glad' when they were reviled and persecuted on earth.

Jesus was sorrowful and troubled, 'even to death', when He considered the separation from the Father's presence which was to take place on the cross. At that time the sins of the world were to be laid upon Him and the Father would have to hide His face. God's wrath would be fully poured out upon Him so that the way would be made for individuals to be reconciled to God.

The events that occurred in the Garden of Gethsemane have implications down through the centuries. The tragedy was that while Jesus was facing this agony, His three closest friends fell asleep. Peter, James and John were tested and they failed. Emotionally exhausted, Jesus turned to his disciples, the very ones who had been so adamant at the Last Supper that they would stand by him. They had fallen asleep and He reproached them. In this terrible moment of mental agony, could they not stay awake? He urged them, instead of sleeping, to pray. Surely they knew how He needed their support? They ought to have been praying for strength for themselves, if not for Him?

Sadly we fail Jesus as the disciples did, so often we think we are strong but the flesh is weak. May we learn a lesson from what happened here and seek to be faithful to our Master.

James' final days

James was present with the other disciples as they gathered to pray. They were all together on the day of Pentecost when the Holy Spirit came upon them. We know little of what James did after this. He obviously had a short ministry career. He suffered a martyr's death about five years after Christ was crucified.

James was put to death during the reign of Herod Agrippa, probably in AD 42. Luke tells us how Herod launched a new persecution of the Christian church. He arrested members of the church and had James put to death, making him the first martyr of the original Twelve (Acts 12:1-3). We do not know why James was chosen to die, when John was just as prominent as James in Jerusalem. We know the Sanhedrin condemned Jesus on false evidence and a similar fate could have happened to James.

We are not given any details in Scripture about James' death but Clement of Alexander gives us his account of a man called Josias who brought a false accusation against James that caused him to be condemned. However, when Josias saw the character and faith of James during his trial, he was moved to declare himself a Christian. As a result both James and Josias were taken away to be beheaded. On the way Josias begged James to forgive him. James paused and said, "Peace be with you," and he kissed the man who had betrayed him. The two men were then beheaded together.

We do not know for certain where James was buried. He may have been buried in Jerusalem by his friends and fellow apostles. It is also possible that his head was buried in Jerusalem but his body was later carried to Spain for safekeeping from the invading Persians. The Spanish have a long tradition that James introduced the Christian faith to Spain where converts were made.

According to tradition, his body was buried at a place called *Santiago de Compostela* (Santiago is Spanish for "James") in northwest Spain and is now the site of a Roman Catholic cathedral.

William Steuart McBirnie in his book *The Search for the Twelve Apostles,* published by Tyndale House, writes: "I for one, having confirmed the fact of the practice of the fragmentation of apostolic relics, and having visited both Spain and Jerusalem, see no reason to doubt the possibility that the bones of James the son of Zebedee are located partly in Spain and partly in Jerusalem to this day."

We may ask why Peter was miraculously delivered from prison by an angel and spared Herod's cruelty, and yet James was martyred. Why are some Christians jailed, tortured and killed while others escape such treatment? These things remain a secret of divine wisdom.

Here we see a man whose character changed under the influence of Jesus Christ. At first the two brothers were called "Boanerges." James wanted to call down curses and fire from heaven on those who rejected His Master, but he changed slowly to a man of peace and silence. He had learned from Jesus to be meek and lowly in heart – can we testify to such a transformation?

James learned to control his temper, bridle his tongue, redirect his zeal, and completely lose his selfish ambition; and the Lord used him to do a great work in the early church.

So let us therefore place our lives, whether they be long like John's or short like James', to the One who is in control of all things and trust Him to bring us safely to that home in heaven He is preparing for His own.

JOHN
THE DISCIPLE WHOM JESUS LOVED

Jesus called James and John as they were preparing the nets in their father Zebedee's boat (Mark 1:19-20). As a result, James and John joined Peter and Andrew as the Master's first disciples. John was one of two disciples who had been with John the Baptist when he proclaimed Jesus as the Lamb of God (John 1:36).

John was the brother of James and younger son of Zebedee and Salome and came from a fishing village along the shores of the Sea of Galilee. Reference in Mark to "hired servants" suggests that they were a well-to-do family and had a successful fishing business (Mark 1:19-20).

The Apostle John is well known to us because he accompanied Jesus in most of the recorded incidents of His ministry. He was one of the inner circle of three - Peter, James and John. He was the author of five New Testament books - the Gospel of John, three Epistles of John, and the Book of Revelation.

When reading Matthew, Mark and Luke, we find that John is nearly always named with Jesus or with Peter or James. Only once does John appear and speak alone. That was when he told Jesus that he had rebuked a man for casting out demons in Jesus name because he was not one of their group of disciples (Mark 9:38).

Jesus gave James and John the nickname "Boanerges," which means Sons of Thunder (Mark 3:17). Some believe this was a reference to their tempers. John became the "beloved disciple" and the only one of the Twelve who did not forsake the Saviour in His hour of death. He stood faithfully at the cross when the Saviour entrusted him to care for His mother (John 19:25-27).

John played a major role in the early church and was at Jesus' side throughout His ministry, witnessing many things including His teaching and miracles. He was present during the Last Supper (John 13:23), was "known to the high priest" (John 18:15), and had outrun Peter to the empty tomb (John 20:2-4). After the resurrection, he became one of the leaders of the early church.

John wanted to stop a man driving out demons

(Mark 9:38-40; Luke 9:49-50)

Jesus and His disciples travelled through Galilee, but He did not wish anyone to know about it. He was teaching His disciples and telling them, "*The Son of Man is going to be betrayed into the hands of men. They will kill Him, and after three days he will rise*" (Mark 9:31).

On the way, the disciples argued among themselves as to who was the greatest. When they reached Capernaum, Jesus asked them what the argument was about on the road, but they remained silent.

However, Jesus knew what it was and called them together and told them, "*If anyone wants to be first, he must be the last and the servant of all.*" The world's philosophy is that you are "great" if others are working for you, but Christ's message is that greatness comes from our serving others. The way to greatness in the kingdom of God is different from the way to greatness in this world.

Then, to emphasise what He was trying to teach His disciples, Jesus set a child before them and took the opportunity to teach them the way to true greatness. Since the words in Aramaic are the same for "child" and "servant," it is not difficult to see why Jesus used this illustration. Jesus was telling His disciples that, instead of arguing as to who was the greatest, they should be humble and take the role of a servant. This was a strong rebuke to the disciples.

This incident was followed by the only recorded words we have of John in the Gospels. He said, *"Teacher, we saw a man driving out demons in your name and we told him to stop, because he was not one of us."* It would appear that not all of Jesus' followers at that time were closely attached to Him, nor were they personally known to the other disciples. At least this one man appears not to have been known or readily recognised by the Twelve.

John had noticed the method used by this man – he was driving out demons in the name of Jesus. John saw that the man had clearly grasped one essential truth, that the Name of Jesus was associated with power to set men free. This is what Jesus had said in His first sermon (Luke 4:16-21).

This does not mean we cannot or should not speak out against unscriptural men and methods, or those who would pervert the truth of the Word of God (Romans 16:17; Jude 3-4). In His rebuke to John, the Lord Jesus indicated that the one they were trying to stop was also serving Him faithfully - just not in the way they thought he should.

John admitted the reason why the disciples had tried to stop the man from driving out the demons was not because of what he was doing, but because he did not belong to their group. Perhaps John had been a little jealous, remembering the time they had tried to remove a demon in Jesus' name and failed. John should have set his pride aside and said, "Praise the Lord," as a man had been healed of demon possession in the name of the Lord.

It is a sad reality that there are those today who will only worship within a select group, denomination, social status, race or doctrinal creed to their own. Naturally, we cannot support the ministry of those who deny the fundamentals of the faith, but within the limits of God's Word, we need tolerance and patience. It is wrong to think that our Denomination or Fellowship is the only true church and all others are misguided and err from the Truth. We are all one in Christ Jesus and every believer is saved by God's grace through faith in the risen Son of God.

John had the attitude that, unless this man was one of the twelve disciples, he should not be doing miracles in Jesus' name. The lesson that John learned about being a godly leader was simply this, 'God also works through other people; we don't have the monopoly on Jesus' name.' Let us therefore check our motives when we inspect the methods and the message of others, who are not part of our group. Everyone needs to be sure of their commitment to Jesus Christ.

"Do not stop him," said Jesus. He then gives two reasons for this pointed rebuke. First, no one who does a miracle in 'the Name of Christ' can, in the next moment, say anything bad about Him. The one relying upon and openly acknowledging the power of the Saviour, for whatever act he performs, must acknowledge Christ. To minister in the Name of Christ, an individual must acknowledge Him as the source of his ministry.

The second reason Jesus gave for His rebuke to John is found in verse 40, *"whoever is not against us is for us."* This teaching can be found in a different form in Matthew 12:30, *"He who is not with me is against me."* Therefore, Jesus is saying, there is no middle ground. Either we are associated with Christ, or we are opposed to Christ.

Perhaps John confessed this incident to Jesus because he was convicted by what was said earlier about the need to be humble and to love one another. Perhaps he was beginning to change his attitude, having been made aware of the lack of love in his life; a lesson that we all need to learn.

John helped to prepare a room for the Passover Supper (Luke 22:8)

For the Jews, the Passover was an annual event to remind them of the night the Children of Israel were delivered out of Egypt (Exodus 12:1-17). The blood of the Passover lamb sprinkled on the door posts would deliver the first-born in that household from the angel of death.

For centuries Israel had kept this feast. Now the Lord Jesus Christ, who was the real Paschal Lamb, was about to be sacrificed, but the disciples were unaware of this. While Jesus was preparing to keep the Passover feast, the Chief Priests and Scribes were plotting how they might kill Him. Little did they realize that He was the Passover Lamb who would die for the sins of the world and open the way for us to enter His kingdom.

The leaders were plotting to kill Jesus and were delighted when one of His disciples offered to betray Him. They agreed to give Judas, who was the one willing to betray Jesus, money and after that he looked for an opportunity to do his evil deed. He thought that no one knew about his plans but Jesus knew all about what he was going to do, as He later revealed.

Jesus said to Peter and John, *"Go and make preparations for us to eat the Passover."* They asked the obvious question, *"Where do you want us to prepare for it?"* He told them to go into the city and they would see a man carrying a jar of water and they were to follow him to his house. This was an unusual sight as normally it was the women who carried water in a jar on their head – if men carried water, it was in a skin not in a jar.

Some have suggested that Jesus deliberately did not tell the disciples the name of the owner of the house or details of where the house could be found, so that Judas would not be able to contact the authorities and have Him arrested before He could observe the Passover. Jesus knew the house where He would be made welcome and could eat the Passover with His disciples. However, Judas would only know the exact location when all the disciples would meet later that evening.

Peter and John would have to purchase a suitable lamb and take it to the Temple to be slain. Then they would take the lamb to the house and have it roasted, and also purchase the necessary unleavened bread, the bitter herbs and wine to prepare the table. No doubt the disciples thought this was going to be a normal annual Passover meal, which they had often celebrated, but it was going to be something far from the usual.

Jesus knew that He had come to the last Passover in which He would participate before fulfilling all He came to accomplish. In this passage, we are reminded four times that the evening before Christ's crucifixion was the time of the Jewish feast when the Passover lamb would be killed. There is no doubt that God planned the death of Jesus, the 'Lamb of God', to coincide with the slaying of the Passover lamb. The death of Christ was the fulfilment of the Passover, His death and shed blood was to make atonement for every sinner all over the world. Paul said, *"Christ, our Passover Lamb, has been sacrificed"* (1 Corinthians 5:7).

Before Jesus and the disciples celebrated the Passover, He got up, wrapped a towel around Himself, and then washed the disciples' feet, including Judas. At first Peter refused to allow Him to wash his feet, but Jesus reminded him that, *"Unless I wash you,*

you have no part with me" (John 13:1-17). When He had finished washing their feet, Jesus explained to them that no one is greater than his master and they should serve one another.

We are told, "*When the hour came, Jesus and his apostles reclined at the table*" (Luke 22:14). Jesus knew so well what was ahead of Him. He had come to the last Passover that God would recognise. He said, "*I tell you I will not drink again of the fruit of the vine until the kingdom of God comes.*" Jesus was now looking beyond His suffering on the cross to the glory that would follow.

After giving thanks, Jesus took the bread, broke it and gave it to them saying, "*This is my body given for you; do this in remembrance of me.*" In the same way He took the cup saying, "*This cup is the new covenant in my blood, which is poured out for you.*" The day of the old covenant was passing away and He was about to seal the new covenant by the shedding of His blood upon the cross. The Lord's Supper is a feast of remembrance, which is still observed by the Church today, when those who partake remember the death of their Saviour and look forward to His coming again.

Once again we see how John, the beloved, was so much involved in this final night. He had helped prepare the Upper Room for the feast, he had prepared the lamb and the table for the Passover and he was reclining close to Jesus. He was also closely involved in the very last encounter with Judas, the one who betrayed his Master.

John in the Garden of Gethsemane

(Matthew 26:36-46; Mark 14:32-42)

John does not record the fact that he was in Gethsemane, but Matthew and Luke state that he was there. Before Jesus went to the cross He, with His disciples, went to Gethsemane to pray. He took Peter, James and John away from the others and instructed them to *"stay here and keep watch."* He then went a little further to be alone while He interceded with His Father about what He was soon to face. When Jesus returned, He found all three asleep and said to them, *"Are you asleep? Could you not watch for one hour? Watch and pray so that you will not fall into temptation. The spirit is willing, but the body is weak."*

John does not record anything of this incident or what happened before Christ's arrest. It may be because it was too sacred and painful for him to record, or he was too ashamed of what he had done. Why did Jesus say, *"My soul is overwhelmed with sorrow to the point of death?"* Why was the Almighty Son of God, who had worked many miracles, so distressed? The sorrow of death - not just physical death but eternal death in the place of the sinner now came upon Him more than ever before. What Jesus endured in Gethsemane has never been experienced by anyone else.

Jesus did not fear death, but faced it with courage and peace. It was not only the physical suffering of death on the cross, horrendous as it was, but the sense of the enormous weight of our sins and transgressions which were laid upon Him. He was being *"made a curse for us."* He was being *"made sin for us who Himself knew no sin."* Surely this shows us how sinful sin must be when we see the agony of our Lord in Gethsemane, even before He went to the cross to bear the punishment for our sins and separation from God.

We cannot put into words how Jesus bore for us the wrath of God in Gethsemane and at Calvary. We deserve to perish in an everlasting hell. There is no doubt this experience must have made an impact upon John. After this, Peter and John followed Jesus to the palace of the High Priest for His trial.

John shows his love and devotion
(John 18:15-16)

John courageously entered the courtyard of the High Priest's palace, though Peter followed afar off. We are not told why and how John was known to the High Priest. It has been suggested that he was known to the High Priest, because of his business connections. It is possible that his father supplied fish to the palace and the High Priest's family or the High Priest knew him because he was a faithful Jew who regularly attended the festivals.

John does not say he was present, but calls himself *"the other disciple."* It is generally believed that it was because of John's humility that he did not record his name. He also wanted to make it clear that what he was recording was true for he was there and saw it.

Through John's influence, he was able to get Peter inside the courtyard. While Peter lingered around the fire, John apparently entered the trial room and remained faithful to Jesus during the interrogation. Peter, after he denied Jesus three times, left in bitter tears.

It is interesting to note only John's Gospel records that John was at the High Priest's house to witness the trial. The other three Gospels only record how Peter was present and denied his Master. John is the only one who tells us how Peter was able to enter the inner court.

This trial was illegal for several reasons: All legal proceedings, including arrests, were forbidden at night. Hebrew law states that arrests and trials leading to capital punishment (death) could not occur at night.

The use of a traitor, and therefore an accomplice, in effecting an arrest or securing a conviction was forbidden by Hebrew law. The arrest of Jesus on the testimony of Judas would make him an accomplice who had aided and abetted Jesus in the propagation of His faith. Therefore, if Judas was an accomplice, Jesus was innocent and His arrest was illegal.

The arrest was not the result of a legal summons. The arrest was the execution of an illegal and factious resolution of the Sanhedrin. The intention was simply to seize a man and do away with him.

According to Hebrew law, it was illegal to bind a man who had not been condemned. After Jesus had been securely bound by the Temple guard in Gethsemane, He was taken to the palace of Annas.

It was against Jewish law for a court to sit on a Sabbath or on a day preceding a Sabbath or a feast day. Yet this trial took place, not only on a day before the Sabbath, but also on a feast day as the feast of Unleavened Bread had begun by the time He was arrested.

It is obvious for these and many other reasons, including the refusal to consider a defence, that the trial was a failure of the officials to do their duty and had surrendered to mob rule.

Christ is proclaimed as the unique Son of God and yet millions today reject Him and refuse to hear any testimony in His favour. They reject the witness of Christians who try to defend their Saviour. One day those who reject the Saviour and refuse to listen to His defence will have to face Him and listen to His words of condemnation on them.

John was present at the Crucifixion

(John 19:16-27)

Of all the disciples, John alone is mentioned as being at Jesus' crucifixion. Where were the other disciples? They had in fact fulfilled the Scripture that says, *"They all forsook Him and fled."* John was standing close enough to the cross for Jesus to see him (John 19:26). He was present to see Jesus nailed to the cross and the moment when a Roman soldier finally pierced His side with a spear.

John was the only one who described the scene when Jesus was on the cross. At the foot of the cross, *"stood his mother, his mother's sister, Mary the wife of Clopas, and Mary of Magdala"* (John 19:25).

Jesus, barely able to speak, instructed John to take care of His mother. We can only assume that Joseph, Jesus' earthly father, had already died and that His brothers or other members of the family were unable to care for her for various reasons – His mother was a believer and, at that time, His brothers did not believe in Him. Therefore, Jesus showed infinite care for His mother, leaving her in the care of His 'beloved disciple,' John.

Surely this is clear evidence that Mary, the mother of Jesus, was an ordinary woman who needed someone to care for her as she got older. It is sad, therefore, when some people honour her as someone who has supernatural powers, who is divine, and who is to be prayed to and worshipped.

Nowhere does the Bible state that Mary was anything but an ordinary human being, whom God chose to use in an extraordinary way. Mary was a righteous woman and favoured (graced) by God (Luke 1:27-28). At the same time, Mary was a sinful human being who needed Jesus Christ as her Saviour, just like everyone else (Romans 3:23; 6.23; 1 John 1:8). Mary recognised that she needed the Saviour.

Nowhere in Scripture has Jesus, or anyone else, directed any praise, glory or adoration towards Mary. Elizabeth, Mary's relative, praised Mary in Luke 1:42-44, but her praise was based on the blessing of giving birth to the Messiah. It was not based on any inherent glory in Mary. The apostles did not give Mary a prominent role. Mary's death is not recorded in the Bible. Nothing is said about Mary ascending to heaven to have an exalted role there. As the earthly mother of Jesus, Mary should be respected, but should not receive our worship or adoration.

The Bible nowhere indicates that Mary can hear our prayers or that she can mediate for us with God. Jesus is our only advocate and mediator in heaven (1 Timothy 2:5). Mary herself sets the example for us, directing her worship, adoration and praise to God alone: *"My soul praises the Lord and my spirit rejoices in God my Saviour, for He has been mindful of the humble state of His servant. From now on all generations will call me blessed, for the Mighty One has done great things for me – holy is His name"* (Luke 1:46-49).

John ran to the empty tomb

(John 20:1-9)

All four Gospels give an account of the empty tomb after Jesus' resurrection. They all mention that it was early on the first day of the week, while Matthew and Mark tell us that the Sabbath was over. John tells us that on the first day of the week, Mary Magdalene went to the tomb early in the morning and found that the stone had been removed from the entrance. The other gospels state she was not the only woman to go to the tomb that morning. At least three other women accompanied her to the tomb with spices to anoint the body of our Lord Jesus Christ. John does not mention the other women's encounter with the empty tomb and the angelic message. Perhaps he was satisfied that there was no need to repeat what would have been generally known through the synoptic writings. He only mentions Mary Magdalene as the one going to the tomb and that, on seeing the stone had been rolled away, she ran to tell Simon Peter and John.

We are then told that Peter and John (John does not refer to himself directly, but only as 'the other disciple') ran to the tomb. John reached the tomb first, bent over and looked in, (the ancient Greek word '*blepo*' is used, which means, "to clearly see a material object, to glance in, to look in"), and saw the strips of linen lying in the tomb.

Peter reached the tomb and immediately went in and saw the strips of linen lying there. (On this occasion the ancient Greek word '*theoreo*' is used which means, "to contemplate, to look carefully, to observe"). It was as if the body had "evaporated" out of the grave clothes.

After Peter went into the tomb, John went in. He saw (the ancient Greek word used was '*eido*' which means, "to understand, to perceive the significance of") and then he believed. The neat, orderly arrangement of the grave clothes showed that this was not a grave robbery; that something absolutely unique had happened in that tomb. John believed that Mary's report was true, and that something awesome and incredibly unique had happened.

John saw the grave clothes wrapped as they had been about Jesus' body, still there in place, but the body was gone. The only way those linen clothes could be left in that condition would be that Jesus passed through them as He arose from the dead. That was all the evidence John saw of the resurrection as he gazed into the tomb, but it led him to be the first disciple to believe that our Lord had risen from the dead. The tomb was empty. There was no dead body there. His quick mind perceived that Jesus was alive. John looked at the evidence. *"He saw, and believed."*

The apostle John's belief in the resurrection was not a "blind leap of faith" when he saw the empty tomb. Jesus had been teaching the disciples that He must be rejected by the religious leaders, be crucified and buried for three days, and then rise from the dead. John was led into a fuller understanding and deeper experience with his Master as he listened and obeyed the teachings of Jesus. However, in spite of this, the resurrection of Jesus surprised him, and all of the disciples. Psychologically they were not prepared for it.

The fact that the tomb was empty and Christ was alive can only be explained as a miracle, a supernatural act of God. There are *"many infallible proofs"* of the bodily resurrection of the Lord Jesus Christ, but the testimony of the empty tomb is the most conclusive of all. Jesus had been buried, with the tomb sealed and guarded by a watch of Roman soldiers. Yet on the third day of His burial, on the morning of the first day of the week, the body was no longer there, and the empty tomb still stands today as an unanswerable proof that the Lord Jesus rose from the dead.

There are other proofs, including the ten or more recorded appearances of the resurrected Christ to His disciples; the amazing change of attitude of the disciples from that of fearful hideaways to fearless evangelists, and the worldwide spread of the Christian faith as founded on the resurrection. As we consider the impact of the resurrection on the world, and on us today, it is helpful to consider its influence on those who first experienced it. We thank Almighty God for the record that John gives of these details.

John the writer

John, who knew Christ very well, was spared for many years to write for the Christian Church as a whole, and for the world at large. John remembered the days and hours when certain events occurred. He was present and could recall what happened at the tenth hour (John 1:39); the seventh hour (John 4:52), and the sixth hour (John 19:14).

John is well known to us as the author of the Gospel of John, the three epistles – First, Second and Third John - and the Book of Revelation. We are privileged to have these writings from the pen of the man who knew Jesus personally, having lived and worked with him for His entire ministry. He saw the miracles Jesus performed; heard every message Jesus spoke; reclined beside Him on that most sacred of all nights, the night of the Last Supper, when it was revealed that Judas was about to betray Jesus. He also stood at the cross, and entered the tomb on that resurrection morning.

The Gospel of John

John never mentions himself by name, not even when listing the apostles, whereas Matthew, Mark and Luke mention his name on many occasions. Someone has said that in the fourth Gospel, John is never visible, and Jesus is never invisible.

John alone speaks of the water being changed into wine, Lazarus being raised from the dead, Jesus talking to the woman of Samaria at the well and Nicodemus coming to Jesus at night. John was one of the chosen three who saw the daughter of Jairus raised and was an eye-witness of the transfiguration.

John wrote as an eye-witness. He said, "*The Word became flesh and lived for a while among us. We have seen his glory, the glory of the one and only Son, who came from the Father, full of grace and truth*" (John 1:14). The Gospel of John has been the means of rich blessing to Christians for centuries.

John wrote what is perhaps the most famous verse in the entire New Testament, *"For God so loved the world, that he gave his one and only Son, that whoever believes in him shall not perish but have eternal life"* (John 3:16). John frequently wrote about love. Some of his more familiar statements of Jesus are: *"A new commandment I give you: Love one another. As I have loved you, so you must love one another. All men will know that you are my disciples if you love one another"* (John 13:34-35). *"If you love me, you will obey what I command"* (John 14:15). *"He who does not love me will not obey my teaching"* (John 14:24).

Some of the best known and best loved texts in the Word of God are found in John's Gospel – words that have been a comfort, a challenge and a blessing to many people down through the generations. *"Do not let your hearts be troubled. Trust in God; trust also in me.* (John 14:1-3,6).

There are also the well known "I am" statements of our Lord - John 6:35; 10:11; 11:25; 15:1. The Gospel of John was written in order that we might believe that Jesus is the Christ. John's love of truth is evident in all his writings. Several very important words frequently occur in his writings – light, life, love, truth, true, witness, believe, world, sign, etc.

Matthew, Mark and Luke are known as the synoptic Gospels because of their similarities in the way that all three look at the life of Christ; but John's Gospel is different as he shows a detailed knowledge of things that the other Gospels omit. John also included important events and teaching that we would not know about if he had not written them down. No one knew Jesus better than John did.

It has been noted by Eusebius that when the three Gospels of Matthew, Mark and Luke were published, John welcomed them and confirmed their accuracy, but remarked that these Gospels omitted to record what Christ had done at the beginning of His ministry. For this reason, John recorded in his Gospel the period that the other Gospels passed over in silence. Therefore, John gives his reason for writing this particular book. He says, *"Jesus did many other miraculous signs in the presence of his disciples, which are not recorded in this book. But these are written that you may believe that Jesus is the Christ, the Son of God, and that by believing you may have life in his name"* (John 20:30-31).

John seems to have presented Jesus' teaching in greater detail than the other evangelists. It was written in Greek for the Gentile believers. It is possible that John laboured on his Gospel for years and that it was released only after his death, when it was prepared for publication by his disciples at Ephesus.

The Epistles of John

John also wrote the three epistles and he tells us, *"I write these things to you who believe in the name of the Son of God so that you may know that you have eternal life"* (1 John 5:13). The epistles were written to people who already believed that Jesus was the Christ, but were not sure of their salvation or knew the assurance of eternal life - *"That you might know"* (1 John 5:13). If you have any doubts as to the life and atoning death of Jesus or of His divinity, read the Gospel of John; but if you have any doubts about assurance, whether you really possess eternal life, then read the epistles of John.

John gives four reasons for writing his First Epistle:

a) The joyful life - *"We write this to make our joy complete"* (1John 1:4).

b) The victorious life - *"I write this to you so that you will not sin"* (1 John 2:1).

c) The prepared life - *"I am writing these things to you about those who are trying to lead you astray"* (1 John 2:26).

d) The life of knowledge - *"I write these things to you who believe in the name of the Son of God so that you may know that you have eternal life"* (1 John 5:13).

In John's Second Epistle, a Christian lady and her family are warned regarding false teachers. He says, *"If anyone comes to you and does not bring this teaching, do not take him into your house or welcome him"* (2 John 1:10). The word "love" occurs four times and the word "truth" five times in this short epistle. The Christian is to "walk in love" and "we are to love one another." He also says, *"It has given me great joy to find some of your children walking in the truth."* Therefore, "walking in the truth" is essential for the Christian life. Love and truth must be maintained in perfect balance. Truth is not to be abandoned in the name of love, but love is not to be displaced in the name of truth.

In his Third Epistle, John is giving instructions on what our behaviour should be towards those who are followers of Christ and who go out proclaiming the truth. Many of the early Christians were called to a life of travelling Evangelists without financial reward, and as a result they were dependent upon the hospitality of the Christians settled in the various towns, villages or cities they passed through. John says, *"It was for the sake of the Name that they went out, receiving no help from the pagans. We ought therefore to show hospitality to such men so that they may work together for the truth"* (3 John, 7-8). The aged apostle wrote to the generous and warm hearted Gaius, commending him for past kindness shown and urging him to continue his most noble work.

The Book of Revelation

John also wrote the book of Revelation which is perhaps the most difficult of all the New Testament books to interpret, primarily because of the elaborate and extensive use of symbolism. The Greek word *apocalypse* is translated "revelation." This English word actually means 'to *reveal*' - not *conceal*. The dictionary definition of *revelation* is: "The act of revealing or disclosing; something revealed, especially a dramatic disclosure of something not previously known or realized."

In other words, Revelation is an open book in which God reveals His plans and purposes to His church. It is the only book of the New Testament that is completely devoted to prophecy. The visions contained in it were given by Christ to His much loved apostle, during his exile on the Isle of Patmos, and were published not long after his death.

John states clearly that Jesus showed him the last vision - "*The Lord, the God of the spirits of the prophets, sent his angel to show his servants things that must soon take place*" (Rev. 22:6).

The early Christians in 96-98 AD, when the book of Revelation was probably written, were about to enter a period of severe persecution. John wrote the book in the first place to steady their faith, and to support those who lived at that time and faced persecution. In God's Word, there is comfort for those who suffer, and for those who agonize over others who suffer.

The Christian Church will not only endure – it will win the battle in the end. Therefore, Revelation was written as an encouragement for the churches that were experiencing a growing hostility towards them and as a warning to the careless and negligent Christians who were tempted to lapse into an easy conformity with the world. Although John wrote this book to the seven churches in Asia Minor, he makes it clear that any believer, who reads the book, and those who obey what was written, will be blessed (Revelation 1:3).

The book was written not only in symbolic language but also in coded language, in order to disguise what was written from those who would be persecuting them. The codes in Revelation were so effective that few people today agree on exactly what John meant.

John was a man who was not afraid to mention God's warnings as well as His promises. On more than one occasion he writes about hell and damnation, while also stressing the depth and security of God's love for His people.

John's final years

When Jesus was on the cross, He asked John to care for His mother. It is believed that John remained in Jerusalem for some years caring for Mary, the mother of Jesus. We do not know for certain how long Mary lived or the place or circumstances of her death. One strong tradition is that she died in Jerusalem. Another tradition points to the city of Ephesus, where she is said to have lived for a while with the apostle John.

John was with Peter at the gate of the Temple when a lame man was healed (Acts 3:10). He was also with Peter on the mission to Samaria when they prayed and laid hands on the new converts to receive the Holy Spirit (Acts 8:14-15). He, along with Peter and James, the Lord's brother, were called "pillars" in the Jerusalem church (Galatians 2:9).

As recorded in Acts 12:1-17, the early Christians were

persecuted by Agrippa I in the year 44 AD. This led to the scattering of the apostles throughout the various Roman provinces of the empire. During this persecution Peter was imprisoned and James was slain. Agrippa I, also known as Herod Agrippa, was the grandson of Herod the Great, recorded in Matthew 2:1, and son of Aristobulus IV and Berenice.

It is possible that John went to Asia Minor at this time and continued to minister God's Word there. John was probably an overseer, during his time in Asia Minor, of the church at Ephesus which had been founded by Paul. From the church at Ephesus other churches were established, together known as the seven churches of Asia Minor, to whom the letters in the first section of the Book of Revelation were written. He returned with the other disciples to Jerusalem for the Apostolic Council (about 51 AD). In Galatians chapter 2, Paul gives an account of his discussions about circumcision and other matters with the 'pillars of the Church', and how they gave Paul and Barnabas the right hand of fellowship. Paul said, *"James, Peter and John, those reputed to be pillars, gave me and Barnabas the right hand of fellowship"* (Galatians 2:9).

However, when Paul came again to Jerusalem to give his report after his second and third missionary journey, he does not mention John as being present (Acts 21:17-26). Some historians draw the conclusion from this that John left Palestine between the years 52 and 55 AD. He was in exile when Jerusalem was destroyed in 70 AD.

There is a tradition that John visited Rome and an attempt was made to poison him but when he took the cup, the poison disappeared in the form of a serpent. Thus the symbol of this apostle is a cup with a serpent coming out of it. John is also traditionally represented as an eagle, usually with a book or scroll, with the first words of the Gospel of John in his beak which stands for the Gospel that he wrote.

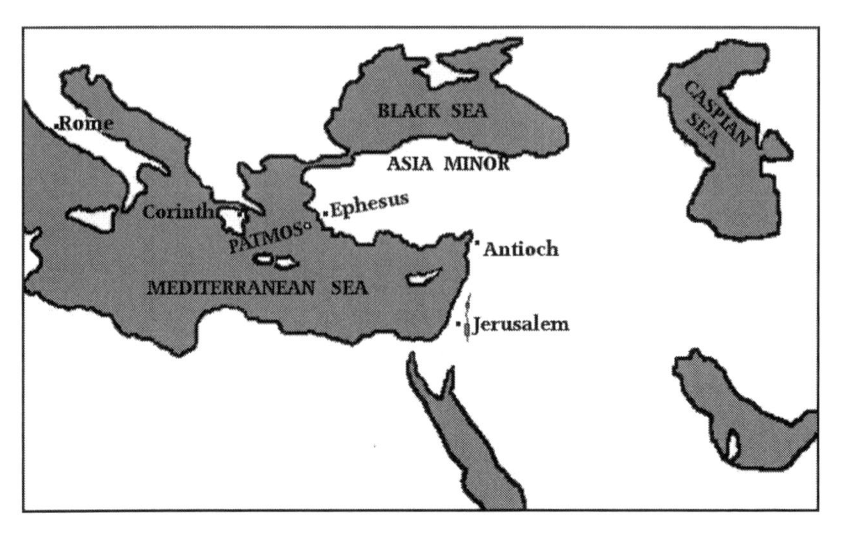

Map of places John visited

In 81 AD, the Emperor Domitian came to power in Rome. He did not take kindly to Christianity and began another persecution in which Philip ultimately lost his life. Once again John escaped death, but he was exiled to a prison on the small island of Patmos where he had remarkable experiences, visions and insights as recorded in the book of Revelation. This is recorded by John in Revelation 1:9. *"I, John, ... was on the island of Patmos because of the word of God and the testimony of Jesus."*

Tradition has it that John was in charge in particular of the churches of Asia Minor, modern Turkey, from 90 to 95 AD. It is thought by some scholars that the Gospel of John and the Epistles of John were written before 95 AD, because in 95 AD there was the extensive persecution and massacre of believers by Domitian. The reason some scholars believe these books were written before this persecution is because there is no reference to it in them. In 96 AD there was a coup, with the result that Domitian was overthrown and killed, and Marcus Cocceius Nerva, who did not persecute the Church, became emperor.

Irenaeus, a native of Asia Minor knew Polycarp who was a disciple of John, together with Eusebius and Clement of Alexander, all claim John lived till the time of Trajan, who became emperor in 98 AD. Apparently John was allowed to leave Patmos and return to Ephesus either during the short reign of Nerva or by Trajan.

When John was old, he trained Polycarp who later became Bishop of Smyrna. This was important because Polycarp was able to carry John's message to future generations. Polycarp taught Irenaeus, and passed on to him stories about John.

John was perhaps the youngest of the disciples when Jesus called him to leave his father's nets and he outlived them all. His brother James was the first to die, being martyred, and John was the last. As a young man, he was very quick and hot-headed but later in life, in his gospel and epistles, he often referred to the need to show love to one another.

John's life was transformed by the presence of Jesus Christ. John, the 'son of thunder,' became John the beloved – an experience that our lives may have when we meet Christ. When we read about John ready to burn up his enemies, we are not likely to predict that he would someday be known as the apostle of love.

In his early years, he was the most unlikely person to be remembered as the apostle of love. But three years with Jesus began to transform a self-centred fanatic into a mature and caring disciple. At first, John portrayed impatience and a lack of genuine love for people. In the incident with the Samaritans, James and John showed a lack of love for unbelievers. John was always committed to truth and there is certainly nothing wrong with that, but it is not enough. Zeal for truth must be balanced by love for people.

John could teach us much about remaining faithful as we grow old. In Joshua 14:8-9 we are told how Caleb, who was eighty-five years old, followed the Lord his God wholeheartedly. Caleb was a man of faith. In spite of the overwhelming odds against him, he followed the Lord and was willing to go to any place, to overcome any problem and even to dream the impossible. Even though Caleb was advanced in years, he said to Joshua, *"Give me this mountain"* (Joshua 14:12).

We need people today, like the apostle John and Caleb, to remain faithful as they grow older; men and women of vision, faith and courage, who are eager to claim great things for Christ and His kingdom.

John was the last remaining apostle to defend Christianity against false teachings and religious and political compromise. He was the last writer of divine truth to be included in the Scriptures. The Book of Revelation, the Gospel of John and the Epistles of John give clear biblical teaching.

According to Jerome, in his final days, John was unable to walk and asked to be carried to church where he addressed the congregation saying, *"Little children, love one another."* Some questioned him why he had so little to say and his reply was, "It is the Lord's command, and if this alone is done, it is enough."

All the disciples, except John, ultimately died for their faith. They were martyred one by one in the prime of life. John was the only disciple who lived to old age and died a natural death. His traditional tomb is thought to be located at Selcuk, a small town in the vicinity of Ephesus.

Simon Peter
the Rock

We have four lists of the twelve apostles in the New Testament: Matthew 10:2-4, Mark 3:16-19, Luke 6:13-16, and Acts 1:13.

In all four biblical lists, the same twelve men are named with a slight variation in the order. In Matthew's record the list of apostles is introduced with the words "first, Simon," followed by Andrew, James and John (Matthew 10:2). Frequently, Simon was the spokesman for the Twelve.

Simon was his personal name but Jesus gave him the name Peter from the Greek '*petros*,' meaning "rock." (Matthew 16:18). Though Peter is most frequently used, there are three other names: Simeon (Hebrew name) (Acts 15:14), Simon, and Cephas (Aramaic for rock), used mostly by Paul (1 Cor. 1:12; 3:22; 9:5; 15:5; Gal. 1:18; 2:9, 11, 14) and one other time in John 1:42. It is obvious that he was called "Simon" throughout Jesus' ministry but came to be known as "Peter" more and more in the apostolic age.

The Gospels provide information about Peter and his family. Peter was the son of a Galilean fisherman, Jonah (Matthew 16:17) or John (John 1:42; 21:15), of whom we have no further knowledge. Peter and his brother Andrew came from Bethsaida (John 1:44) in the province of Galilee and were Galilean fishermen (Mark 1:16; Luke 5:2–3; John 21:3). Peter was married (Mark 1:30; Luke 4:38) and lived in Capernaum (Mark 1:21–31). Simon and his brother Andrew were partners with James and John in a fishing business in Capernaum (Luke 5:9-10).

In Jesus' day, Capernaum was the major town on the north tip of the Sea of Galilee. For several months Jesus made Capernaum His home and the base of His ministry. Jesus seems to have been very popular in Capernaum. In fact, when He returned to Nazareth, His home town, the people said, *"Do here in your home town what we have heard that you do in Capernaum"* (Luke 4:23). However, Jesus announced *"woe"* on both Bethsaida and Capernaum (Matthew 11:21-24). Those cities are in ruins today.

Peter left everything to follow Jesus

(Matthew 4:18–20; Mark 1:16-18; Luke 5:1–11; John 1:35-42)

The Gospels give us three different accounts of Peter coming to Jesus, reflecting the different points that the Gospel writers thought important or wished to emphasize.

The first account is found in John 1:35-42 where Andrew had heard John the Baptist declare of Jesus, *"Look, the Lamb of God!"* As a result, Andrew followed Jesus. This was an account of Andrew coming to faith in Jesus Christ, recognising Him to be the *"Lamb of God, who takes away the sin of the world."* The first thing Andrew did was to find his brother Simon and take him to Jesus. This is an example of what all Christians should do – tell their friends about Jesus. As soon as Jesus saw Simon, He said to him, *"You are Simon son of John. You will be called Cephas."* As a result of this meeting Peter also believed in Jesus.

The second account is found in Matthew 4:18-20 and Mark 1:16-18. It is recorded that Jesus was walking beside the Sea of Galilee when He saw Simon, with his brother Andrew, casting a net into the sea. Jesus called them saying, *"Come, follow me, and I will make you fishers of men."* We are told that they immediately left their nets and followed Jesus.

The third account is given in Luke 5:1-11. On this occasion a large crowd gathered around Jesus, so He got into a boat and taught the people from it. Later Jesus asked Simon to move away from the shore to catch some fish. But Simon argued that they had been fishing all night and had caught nothing. However, he obeyed Jesus' request and moved out. Soon they caught so many fish that they had to call their friends to come with their boat to help with the catch. When Simon saw the catch of fish, he fell on his knees and said, *"Go away from me, Lord; for I am a sinful man!"* Then Jesus said to Simon, *"Don't be afraid; from now on you will catch men."* Then we are told, *"They pulled their boats up on shore, left everything and followed him."*

These accounts agree that Peter became a committed disciple of Jesus.

The healing of Peter's mother-in-law

(Matthew 8:14–15; Mark 1:29–31; Luke 4:38–39)

After Jesus healed the demon-possessed man in the synagogue in Capernaum, He and His disciples went to the home of Simon Peter and Andrew.

When they reached the house, Jesus was told that Peter's mother-in-law was ill. Matthew and Mark tell us that she was *"in bed with a fever"* and Luke, who was a doctor, tells us that she was *"suffering from a high fever."* Jesus was taken to her and, in Mark's account, He went and took her by the hand and raised her up. Luke states that Jesus "rebuked" the fever. These accounts do not conflict. Each writer chose to emphasize different details of the story in order to reveal a different characteristic of Jesus.

The Greek word for "rebuked" (*epetimesan*) is the same word that is used to describe how Jesus cast out the demon in the synagogue (Luke 4:35). We do not know the cause of this fever but the fact that it was high and that the woman was too sick to get up, suggest an extremely serious and perhaps life threatening illness.

What we have before us in the accounts of this miracle, in reality, is a double miracle. First of all, Jesus took her by the hand, lifted her up and the fever immediately left her. The second aspect of the miracle according to Dr. Luke was that she was immediately given a complete restoration of her strength. In all the accounts, the effect was immediate; the fever not only left her, but she was able to "serve them."

From this incident of the healing of Peter's mother-in-law, we should observe that Peter was a married man. At a later period, his wife accompanied him on his evangelistic journeys. Some churches teach that their Pastor/Priest should not marry but the requirement of celibate ministry conflicts with what God has permitted. The apostle Paul clearly states, "*Don't we have the right to take a believing wife along with us, as do the other apostles and the Lord's brothers and Cephas?*" (1 Corinthians 9:5). Word spread about Jesus and those who had seen the miracles of Jesus told others.

Later in Mark's Gospel, we are told of another great miracle when a dead girl was restored to life. Here we see that sickness and death comes to everyone. Peter's mother-in-law had just been healed from a fever. Now we have Jesus healing the daughter of Jairus who was a 'ruler.' Jairus probably had wealth and could afford to pay for medical treatment for his daughter but no amount of money could prevent her death. There is no distinction, class or creed in sickness and death. Peter, along with James and John, were present at the raising of Jairus' daughter (Mark 5:37; Luke 8:51).

Peter walked on the water

(Matthew 14:22-34; Mark 6:45-53; John 6:16-21)

Jesus, having multiplied bread and fish enough to satisfy a crowd of five thousand men plus women and children, went off by Himself to pray. He instructed the Twelve to cross by boat to the other side of the Sea of Galilee. In the fourth watch, just before dawn, when the apostles' boat was far out on the lake and they were battling against a strong wind and rough sea, they saw a figure approaching them, walking on the surface of the lake. Terrified, they thought they were seeing a ghost. Matthew tells us that they *"cried out in fear"* (Matthew 14:26).

John tells us that the boat was over three miles out from the shore at that time (John 6:19). Mark tells us that Jesus could see the disciples from where He sat praying on the mountainside (Mark 6:48). The disciples were having a hard time rowing because a strong wind was blowing against them.

Identifying Himself, Jesus said, "*Take courage! It is I. Don't be afraid.*" Impulsively Simon cried out, "*Lord, if it's you, tell me to come to you on the water.*" Jesus replied, "*Come.*" Peter got out of the boat and began walking on the water toward Jesus. But when Peter took his eyes off Jesus and saw the wind and waves, he began to panic and started to sink. Peter cried out to the Lord, "*Lord, save me*" and Jesus immediately reached out His hand and caught Peter, saying, "*You of little faith, why did you doubt?*" As they climbed into the boat together, the storm died down. Then the disciples worshipped Jesus, saying, *"Truly you are the Son of God"* (Matt. 14:27-33).

Was the storm a surprise to Jesus? No. Jesus sent them out knowing this storm was coming for a reason. He wanted to test their faith, and teach them something new about Himself.

The disciples, even though they had spent much time with Jesus, did not recognize Him in the storm. Sometimes we do not recognize the Lord when He comes to us in the middle of our "storms." Peter did not begin to sink until he started looking around at the wind and the waves. This highlights the danger of taking our eyes off Jesus and allowing our focus to be dominated by the difficulties that threaten us.

Peter was an extraordinary man. He was the boldest of all the disciples. The other disciples may have been challenged about walking on the water but were afraid to suggest such a thing, while Peter was the only one who dared request Jesus to ask him to come to Him. Peter had enough faith to step out of the protection of the boat in the dark, as the wind was whipping up the waves.

Peter started out full of confidence and with good intentions, but his faith wavered. At first Peter's eyes were fixed on Jesus and he did not look at the rough sea. His faith was strong as he focused on Jesus, *"but when he saw the wind, he was afraid and, beginning to sink, cried out, 'Lord, save me'"* (Matthew 14:30).

Peter had an awareness of the One who could save him from his desperate situation and in response to Peter's cry, Jesus came to the help of the frightened disciple as he reached out to rescue him. Jesus is still the one who is ready to respond to our cries for help. When we call out to Jesus, He reaches out His hand and helps us in those trying situations. We are told when Jesus got into the boat, "the wind died down." When we have Jesus "in our boat" the storms of life will be calmed and we can worship Him.

Peter's confession of Christ

(Matthew 16:13-20; Mark 8:27-30; Luke 9:18-21)

Just before Peter's confession, the Pharisees asked for a sign from Jesus, a request that He found distressing. *"He sighed deeply and said, 'Why does this generation ask for a miraculous sign?'"* Jesus refused saying, *"I tell you the truth, no sign will be given to it"* (Mark 8:12). Instead, He left them and got into a boat and travelled to the other side of the lake (Mark 8:13). This was not the first time that He had withdrawn from those who opposed Him.

After the trip to the other side of the lake, Jesus warned the disciples of *"the yeast of the Pharisees"* (Mark 8:14-21). The Pharisees tried to correct Jesus with their own man-made laws that were not from Moses. Jesus' whole ministry was in conflict with their teachings and, more often than not, He was addressing the laws that they afflicted upon the people. They were very religious and wanted everyone to learn and follow their ways and interpretations of the Scripture.

The Pharisees did all their good deeds and their spiritual obligations in front of people as much as possible. They said long and loud prayers publicly (on the street). They gave their money (frequently having a horn blown when they gave their tithes) and did their good works openly, as they wanted to be seen and looked for the recognition of men.

The Pharisees demanded to see Jesus perform miracles and would not consider believing in Him without witnessing one. *"The Pharisees and Sadducees came to Jesus and tested him by asking him to show them a sign from heaven"* (Matthew 16:1). Jesus' response was, *"A wicked and adulterous generation looks for a miraculous sign, but none will be given it except the sign of Jonah"* (v.4).

To fully appreciate the answer Jesus gave, we must go to the Old Testament book of Jonah. In Jonah 1:1-17, we read that God commanded the prophet Jonah to go to the city of Nineveh and warn its people that He was going to destroy it for its wickedness. Jonah disobeyed the Lord and headed, in the opposite direction, for the city of Tarshish by boat. The Lord then sent a severe storm that caused the crew of the ship to fear for their lives. Jonah was thrown overboard and swallowed by a great fish where he remained for "*three days and three nights*." After the three-day period, the Lord caused the great fish to vomit Jonah out onto dry land (Jonah 2:10).

It is this three-day statement that Jesus was referring back to when He spoke of the sign of Jonah. Jesus had already been performing miracles that were witnessed by many. Jesus had just performed a great sign in the Pharisees' presence by healing a deaf man who was possessed of a demon. Rather than believe, they accused Jesus of doing this by the power of Satan. Jesus recognized their hardness of heart and refused to give them further proof of His identity. However, He did say that there would be one further sign forthcoming, His resurrection from the dead after being in the tomb for three days. This would be their final opportunity to be convinced.

When the disciples and Jesus reached the other side of the lake, they came to Bethsaida, where Jesus healed a blind man. Jesus instructed the healed man not to return to the village (Mark 8:22-26). This was not the first time that Jesus indicated that He did not want publicity. Jesus refused to offer signs to the religious leaders and instead departed from them, crossing the lake to get away.

This is the background to Peter's confession, as after these events, Jesus asked his disciples, "*Who do people say I am?*" (Mark 8:27). The disciples told Him what people were saying about Him - John the Baptist from the dead, Elijah, Jeremiah, or one of the old prophets back from the dead.

It is true that it had been prophesied Elijah would come again, *"See, I will send you the prophet Elijah before that great and dreadful day of the Lord comes"* (Malachi 4:5). Did those who studied the scriptures think that Jesus was the fulfilment of this prophecy? It was John the Baptist who came *"in the spirit and power of Elijah"* (Luke 1:17). But Jesus wanted the personal opinions of the disciples saying, *"But what about you? Who do you say I am?"* (Matthew 16:15).

Without hesitation, Peter replied, *"You are the Christ, the Son of the living God"* (v. 16). Jesus declared that Simon received this revelation from His heavenly Father, then pronounced a blessing on him, *"You are Peter, and on this rock I will build my church, and the gates of Hades will not overcome it"* (v. 18).

It is very important that we have a right understanding of who Jesus is. Who He is, and what He can do, go together and are essential for our salvation (Romans 10:9-10; 1 John 4:1-3). Jesus said that Peter's declaration had been revealed to him by His heavenly Father.

This was not the first time a similar confession had been made: when Jesus revealed to Nathanael that He had seen him under the fig tree before Philip found him, Nathanael declared, *"Rabbi, you are the Son of God; you are the King of Israel"* (John 1:49). Also, when Jesus walked on the water to be with His disciples who were in a boat during a storm, Peter declared, *"Truly you are the Son of God"* (Matthew14:33). When Andrew brought his brother Simon to Jesus it was because of his conviction as to who Jesus was, *"We have found the Messiah"* (John 1:41). Peter gave a confession of faith at a time when the crowds left Jesus after His sermon on the Bread of Life, *"You have the words of eternal life. We believe and know that you are the Holy One of God"* (John 6:68).

However, this confession of Peter was different from the

others. It was not through human intellect or merit that Peter confessed Christ to be the Messiah. After all, "*no one can say, 'Jesus is Lord,' except by the Holy Spirit*" (1 Corinthians 12:3). Only God can reveal His Son to the human mind. Jesus said, "*No one knows the Son except the Father, and no one knows the Father except the Son and those to whom the Son chooses to reveal him*" (Matthew 11:27). Only by divine revelation can we know Christ.

Peter was able to make his announcement about Jesus' identity because God had enabled him to recognize Jesus as "*the Christ, the Son of the living God.*" "*This was not revealed to you by man, but by my Father in heaven*" (Matthew 16:16-17). At this point in Matthew's Gospel, Jesus gave Simon the name Peter. "*I tell you that you are Peter, and on this rock I will build my church, and the gates of Hades will not overcome it*" (Matthew16:18). Matthew wrote his Gospel for a Jewish audience. He expected his readers to be familiar with Old Testament imagery.

Mark's Gospel records he was given the name Peter when Jesus called him (Mark 3:16). Likewise in John's account, Jesus gave him the name Peter at their first encounter (John 1:42). Peter was a Jew and with his knowledge of the Old Testament would know that '*Rock*' throughout the Hebrew Scripture is never used symbolically of man, but always of God. In the Old Testament God is referred to as a Rock: "*He is the Rock, his works are perfect*" (Deuteronomy 32:4). In the Psalms, David continually wrote of the Rock, not as if it represented a man, but clearly as a representation of God, "*The Lord is my rock, my fortress and my deliverer; my God is my rock, in whom I take refuge*" (Psalm 18:2); "*For who is God besides the Lord? And who is the Rock except our God?*" (Psalm 18:31). David makes it clear that '*God alone*' is the true Rock in whom we should put our trust for salvation, "*My soul finds rest in God alone; my salvation comes from him. He alone is my rock and my salvation ...*" (Psalm 62:1-2).

Throughout the Bible, the concept of "the Rock" has always referred to God, and to Christ. The apostle Paul clearly defined the "Rock" that gave water to the children of Israel in the days of Moses: "... *they drank from the spiritual rock that accompanied them, and that rock was Christ*" (1 Corinthians 10:4).

What Jesus said to Peter could be translated, 'You are *Stone*, and upon this *bedrock* I will build My church.' His choice of words would indicate that the rock on which the church would be built was something other than Peter.

When using *Petros* as "a movable stone," Jesus is using a word with a double meaning. In Matthew 16:18 Jesus says to Simon, "*you are Petros (a moveable stone) and upon this Petra (a large unmoveable rock) I will build my Ekklesia" (Assembly).* The meaning is that Petros is just one stone in an assembly of stones. The assembly is built on the immoveable Rock that is Jesus.

This was the understanding of the early Christians, and there is no record either in the Bible or in early church history that Peter was considered the "infallible" head of the Christian church. Yet, the question remains: Why did Jesus say what He did to Peter?

For centuries, there have been those who have maintained that Jesus Christ founded His church upon the Apostle Peter, and that the office and jurisdiction of the bishop of Rome represents an "unbroken" line of apostolic succession from Peter to the present day. There are those who interpret Jesus as saying, "You are Peter, and upon you, Peter, I will build My church." Peter would be the rock upon which the Church would be built. He would be the "prince of all the apostles and the visible head of the whole church."

There are several difficulties with this explanation. The first is when we look at the Greek of Matthew 16:18, we see something that is not obvious in the English. Jesus said, "*You are Peter (Petros), and upon this rock (petra) I will build My church."* The Greek word *"petros"* is masculine and *"petra"* is feminine. The first word *petros,* means a fragment of stone chipped from the rock-face; the second word *petra,* implying the whole rock itself.

Jesus said that the rock He would build His church on was not the masculine "*petros*" but the feminine "*petra.*"

What, then, is the true significance of our Lord's word about building His Church on a 'Rock'? The two Greek words used indicate the Lord was talking about two distinct things. His choice of words would show that the rock on which the church would be built was something other than Peter. "This rock" that the church is built on is not Peter, but the confession Peter made, "*You are the Christ, the Son of the living God.*" Jesus replied, "*Blessed are you, Simon son of Jonah, for this was not revealed by man, but by my Father in heaven*" (Matthew 16:16-17).

"*And I tell you that you are Peter (petros), and on this rock (petra) I will build My church, and the gates of Hades will not overcome it.*" Interpreting Christ as the rock upon which the church would be built also agrees with other statements in Scripture. Paul warned, "*For no-one can lay any foundation other than the one already laid, which is Jesus Christ*" (1 Corinthians 3:11). Here, he emphasizes that Christ is the foundation upon which the church is built. In Ephesians, Paul speaks of the church as having been "*built on the foundation of the apostles and prophets, with Christ Jesus himself as the chief corner stone*" (Ephesians 2:20). Here Paul pictures Christ as the '*chief corner stone*' and the apostles and prophets as secondary stones.

If Peter is the rock on which Christ was to build His church, Peter could not be overcome and the gates of hell could not prevail against him. But the fact is that he was overcome, and the gates of hell did prevail against him. Didn't he deny his Lord? This was after

Christ told him that the Rock was not to be overcome. Jesus told Peter on one occasion: *"Out of my sight, Satan! You are a stumbling block to me; you do not have in mind the things of God, but the things of men"* (Matthew 16:23).

If the church was built on Peter, then Peter would be the head of the church. However, Peter was not the head of the church in his day. Jesus said: "*You are not to be called 'Rabbi', for you have only one Master and you are all brothers. And do not call anyone on earth 'father', for you have one Father, and he is in heaven. Nor are you to be called 'teacher' for you have one Teacher, the Christ .... For whoever exalts himself, will be humbled"* (Matthew 23:8-12).

It is clear the forbidding of the calling anyone on earth 'father' relates to spiritual fathers rather than earthly fathers. Jesus in his teaching reinforced the fifth commandment to fully respect earthly parents in Mark 7:10.

If Jesus appointed Peter as the head of the church, why did the other disciples quarrel among themselves as to who would be the greatest (Luke 9:46)? If this decision had already been made by Christ, why should the others be anxious about it? The other disciples would have submitted to the wish of their Master. Therefore, it seems clear that no such appointment had been made by Jesus.

Neither Peter nor any of his successors were head of the true church. There is no man on this earth who is the head of the Church. The Lord Jesus Christ and He alone, is the head of His body which is the Church. He says very plainly that there is no remedy for sin, and there is no salvation, except through faith in the Lord Jesus Christ. God the Father sent Jesus into the world, as Peter said, *"He himself bore our sins in his own body on the tree"* (1 Peter 2:24).

Paul explains this when he says, *"The head of every man is Christ"* (1 Cor. 11:3). God *"placed all things under his feet and appointed him to be head over everything for the church, which is his body"* (Ephesians 1:22). As we look at the context, this explains that Jesus is the head of every person and also of the church. We are responsible to the head, which is Christ, and not to men who try to mislead the work of Christ and take His place.

The context of Matthew 16:13-20 is not about Peter; it is about Jesus. It starts with a question that Jesus raised about His identity: *"Who do people say that the Son of Man is?"* (Matthew 16:13). It reached a climax with Peter's declaration: *"You are the Christ, the Son of the living God"* (Matthew 16:16). It concludes with the Lord warning His disciples *"not to tell anyone that He was the Christ"* (Matthew 16:20).

Peter with Jesus at the Transfiguration

(Matthew 17:1-13; Mark 9:2-13; Luke 9:28-36)

Only Matthew, Mark and Luke record the incident of Jesus taking Peter, James and John up a high mountain where He was transfigured before them. This was one of the most moving events in Peter's life. We do not know why John did not record this remarkable experience that was witnessed by only three of our Lord's disciples.

Jesus was transfigured before their eyes and His clothes became dazzling white. Elijah appeared to them along with Moses. These Old Testament characters were in conversation with Jesus (Mark 9:2-4).

Peter, as usual, was the spokesman for the small group. However, the astonishing thing he witnessed meant he struggled to respond appropriately and he made a surprising suggestion, saying, "*Rabbi, it is good for us to be here. Let us put up three shelters – one for you, one for Moses and one for Elijah*" (Mark 9:5). Peter was obviously so overcome by what he saw that he wanted to preserve the experience by building three tents for worship on the site. Before he could say anything more "*A cloud appeared and enveloped them, and a voice came from the cloud: 'This is my Son, whom I love. Listen to him!' Suddenly, when they looked round, they no longer saw anyone with them except Jesus*" (Mark 9:7-8).

As they came down from the mountain, Jesus instructed them not to tell anyone what they had seen until after His resurrection. This experience made such an impact upon Peter that many years later he wrote about it in his letter of 2 Peter 1:16-19. Here, Peter speaks of the importance of the Transfiguration to him. He obviously was perplexed about Jesus' talk of suffering and death. However, when he saw the greatest personalities of the Old Testament talking with Jesus, he came to understand that the prophecies about Jesus' suffering and death were true and reliable.

What did this mean? Surely it was a lesson for the disciples about who Jesus was. The disciples (Peter speaking for them) had confessed that Jesus was the Messiah, but they had a mistaken idea of what that meant, and Jesus speaking of His death had confused them. The Transfiguration served to confirm Peter's confession. It showed to Peter, James and John that Jesus was no ordinary man nor even a great prophet, but that He was indeed no less than the Son of God, the Messiah of Israel. God was confirming the disciples' confession.

In the Transfiguration, the three selected disciples saw a foretaste of the glory and victory of Jesus. This would become even clearer to them after Jesus' resurrection, and it was really only then that the disciples began to understand what Jesus had been teaching. This scene encouraged the disciples and showed them that Jesus was indeed the Son of God.

This scene would also help them to understand about the cross of Jesus and His commitment to it. In Luke's version of the story, he tells us that Jesus spoke with Moses and Elijah about His approaching death in Jerusalem (Luke 9:31). This is an important piece of information, for it shows us the proper context in which to view this incident. The series of events, as told in Matthew, also show us very plainly that the Transfiguration was meant to be interpreted in the context of the death and resurrection of Jesus. References to Jesus' death literally surround the Transfiguration story (Matthew 16:21; 17:12, 22-23), and Jesus told His disciples not to discuss what they had seen until after His resurrection (Matthew 17:9). Clearly, the Transfiguration contained a crucial message about Jesus' identity and mission and Jesus wanted the disciples to recall the incredible event after his glorious resurrection.

Jesus wanted His disciples to know that He would be glorified, but not in the way most people were expecting - a worldly kind of honour, or by making war with Rome. The glory that was awaiting Jesus, which the disciples had just experienced in a glimpse of Jesus in the Transfiguration, would come through His death and resurrection. The Transfiguration was therefore meant to be a lesson on the cross, to show its necessity. It would only be through His death and resurrection that He would attain glory. That is why Jesus committed Himself to the cross: it was the path to glory (cf. John 12:24).

The Transfiguration cleared away all Peter's doubts. When he saw the greatest prophets of the Old Testament worshipping the glorified Jesus, Peter realised that all prophecy spoke of Jesus and His destiny to suffer and die.

The purpose of the Transfiguration of Christ was so that the "inner circle" of His disciples could gain a greater understanding of who Jesus was. Christ underwent a remarkable change in appearance in order that the disciples could see Him in His glory. The disciples, who had only known Him in His human body, now had a greater realization of the deity of Christ, though they could not fully understand it. That gave them the assurance they needed after hearing the sad news of His coming death.

Peter and the other disciples who were present never forgot what happened that day on the mountain. Many years later he wrote how Jesus *"received honour and glory from God the Father when the voice came to him from the Majestic Glory, saying, 'This is my Son, whom I love; with him I am well pleased.' We ourselves heard this voice that came from heaven when we were with him on the sacred mountain"* (2 Peter 1:17-18).

Jesus washed Peter's feet

(John 13:1–17)

In the first century, walking on the dusty roads of Palestine made it very important that feet were washed before a communal meal. Since people reclined at a low table their feet were exposed. When Jesus rose from the table and began to wash the feet of the disciples, He was doing the work of the lowliest of servants.

The disciples must have been very surprised by this act of humility from their Master. It would have been entirely appropriate for the disciples to wash their master's feet, but not Jesus to wash their feet.

This act of humility by Jesus was in direct contrast to that of the disciples, who had recently been arguing among themselves as to which of them was the greatest (Luke 22:24). Obviously, there was no servant present to wash their feet and apparently it did not occur to them to wash one another's feet.

When the Lord Himself stooped to carry out this humble task, the disciples must have been embarrassed. We do not know whose feet Jesus started to wash. Peter found it too much when Jesus came to him and was not happy that the Lord should wash his feet, saying, "*No, you shall never wash my feet.*" Jesus' reply to him was, "*Unless I wash you, you have no part with me.*" With that, Peter made a complete turn around and demonstrated his love for his Master by saying, "T*hen Lord, not just my feet but my hands and my head as well!*" Then Jesus went on to explain, "*A person who has had a bath needs only to wash his feet; his whole body is clean. And you are clean, though not every one of you.*"

In those days, a rich man had a large bath in the centre court of his house and when he arose in the morning he had a bath and was made completely clean. However, during the day he would walk on the dusty ground wearing sandals, causing his feet to become dirty, and when he returned home a servant would wash them. He did not need a bath every time he came in as only his feet needed washing. However, it is now clear that Jesus has turned the conversation around and was not talking about physical dirt, but about sin and the need to be cleansed from it.

The image here is clear for the believer. When we receive Jesus as our personal Saviour, He forever washes us from our sins (John 3:16; 1 John 5:13). We have been eternally cleansed from head to toe through His cleansing blood. However, as we walk through life, we tend to fall into sin and so we need cleansing; not for the entire person, since that was accomplished when we were saved, but just for that particular sin which we committed in our daily walk. Jesus is teaching us that we do not need to repeat getting saved every time we sin, but we do need to come to Him for forgiveness and restoration of fellowship. If we keep on sinning, we further break the fellowship between us and the Lord. The secret to true spiritual joy is the practice of instant confession of sins and failures before the throne of grace. We need a heart like David's who said, "*I acknowledged my sin to you and did not cover up my iniquity. I said, 'I will confess my transgressions unto the Lord' and you forgave the guilt of my sin*" (Psalm 32:5).

Salvation is a one-time act of justification by faith. In justification, Christ paid the debt for our sins – no-one can condemn us for God has justified us. When we become Christians, sanctification begins in our lives. Sanctification is a lifelong growing process as we daily walk through life with our Saviour and seek His cleansing. Peter and the disciples - all except Judas, who never belonged to Christ - needed this daily cleansing.

When we come to Christ for the washing of our sins, we can be sure that it is permanent and complete. No act can cleanse us further from our sin, as our sin has been exchanged for the perfect righteousness of Christ on the cross (2 Corinthians 5:21). But we do need continual cleansing from the effects of living in the flesh in a sin-cursed world.

It is important to note that, while Jesus said the disciples were clean, He also knew the condition of Judas. He said, "*You are clean, though not every one of you. For he knew who was going to betray him, and that was why he said not every one was clean*" (John 13.10-11).

When Jesus finished washing the feet of the disciples, He put His outer garment on again, returned to His place at the table and began to explain to the disciples what He had done. He had shown them humility and the need for God's people to take a servant role. Jesus told them, "*I have set you an example that you should do as I have done for you*" (John 13:15). "*Now that you know these things, you will be blessed if you do them*" (John 13:17).

Peter denied knowing Jesus

(Matthew 26:31-35, 69-75; Mark 14:27-31, 66-72; Luke 22:31-34, 54-62; John 13:36-38, 18:15-18, 25-27)

After Jesus and His disciples left the Upper Room, where they had celebrated the Last Supper, they made their way to the Mount of Olives. On the way Jesus said to them, "*This very night you will all fall away on account of me, for it is written: 'I will strike the shepherd, and the sheep of the flock will be scattered*" (Matthew 26:31).

Each of the four accounts gives us slightly different information about Peter's predicted denial of Jesus. In Matthew, Peter said, "*Even if I have to die with you, I will never disown you.*" Mark's Gospel has the same words but records that, "*Peter insisted emphatically*" when saying them (Mark 14:31). Then in Luke we read that Jesus told Peter that, "*Satan has asked to sift you as wheat. But I have prayed for you ......*" Peter replied, "*Lord, I am ready to go with you to prison and to death*" (Luke 22:31-33). Then in John's Gospel we read that Peter asked, "*Lord, why can't I follow you now? I will lay down my life for you*" (John 13:37).

Jesus told His disciples that He was going where they could not follow (He was going to the cross). Peter asked, "*Lord where are you going?*" Jesus informed Peter that where He was going it would not be possible for him to follow at that time, but he would follow later (Peter would later be crucified upside down).

Then Jesus turned to Peter and made a remarkable statement, "*I tell you the truth, this very night, before the cock crows, you will disown me three times*" (Matthew 26:34). Rather than taking this rebuke to heart and examining himself to be careful about his life, this only brought more boasting from Simon, "*Even if I have to die with you, I will never disown you*" (Matthew 26:35). All the other disciples said the same.

Simon did not think it possible that he could ever deny his Master. The other disciples were of the same opinion. Jesus had predicted that all His followers would run away. Why would they flee? Perhaps fear of being arrested or fear of being killed. After a few hours, all of their brave talk and promises were apparently forgotten, for we are told that after Jesus was arrested, "*All the disciples deserted him and fled*" (Matthew 26:56).

What went wrong? Peter had started out well that night, determined to follow Jesus, even to death. Then, before he knew what was happening, he was cursing and denying Jesus.

At first, Peter was sitting in the courtyard and a servant girl accused him of being "*with Jesus of Galilee.*" Peter denied it saying, "*I don't know what you're talking about.*" Then he went out to the gateway where another girl saw him and said to the people there, "*This fellow was with Jesus of Nazareth.*" This time Peter "*denied it again, with an oath: I don't know the man.*" This raised some curiosity among those standing around and said, "*Surely you are one of them, for your accent gives you away.*" This time Peter went further and "b*egan to call down curses on himself and he swore to them, 'I don't know the man!'*" (Matthew 26:69-74).

While in the courtyard, three people said something about Peter's relationship to Jesus - only one of the accusations was said directly to Peter himself; the other two accusations were said to the crowd around the fire. In response, Peter denied knowing the Lord. What happened? What pushed him over the edge? Was he overwhelmed by what was happening around him? Perhaps he felt isolated and intimidated by the sudden change of events and panicked.

The Bible does not tell us what caused Peter to suddenly change from a courageous and confident man, who was prepared to die with Jesus, to be a weak individual who denied his Master when questioned by a little servant girl. Whatever the cause of his failure, it was wrong, and shows us the frailty of our humanity. The apostle Paul reminds us, "*If you think you are standing firm, be careful that you don't fall!*" (1 Corinthians 10:12).

We notice something about Peter; he followed at a distance when he should have been at Jesus' side. Why did Peter follow at a distance? Why did Peter deny knowing the Lord? One commentator put it this way: Peter followed out of love, but at a distance out of fear. Peter perhaps had a good reason to fear. After all, he wounded the servant of the high priest and cut off his ear, and now he was in the courtyard with that high priest.

The cock crowed and Peter had denied the Lord three times. Jesus turned around and looked straight at Peter. Then Peter remembered the Lord's statement about disowning Him three times, broke down and wept bitterly, he had let the Lord down. He had broken his promise and had denied the Lord. In the space of a few hours, Jesus was betrayed by Judas and denied by Peter.

The wonderful news is that there was a happy ending for Peter, not like Judas. Peter was restored, which gives us hope. When Jesus arose from the dead the angel at the empty tomb said to the women, "*Go, tell the disciples and Peter*" (Mark 16:7). After the resurrection, Jesus came to Peter and the others at the Sea of Tiberias where they had been fishing (John 21:1-14).

As we look at Peter and see the collapse of his own confidence, his boasting and pride, we see how we too can find strength, not in ourselves, but in the One who loved us and died for us. Jesus made a promise to restore Peter's faith and He did. He returned Peter to the fold. He used Peter as a leader in the early church to strengthen and encourage the other disciples and followers.

The Good News of the Gospel is that the Lord remains faithful to us even when we, like Peter, fail and fall. He keeps forgiving us and restoring us to His fold.

Peter ran to the empty tomb

(Luke 24:12; John 20:3-10)

The resurrection of Jesus was totally unexpected by Christ's followers. When Peter and John heard what Mary had to say about the body of Jesus being taken out of the tomb, they wasted no time in going to investigate. Peter ran as fast as he could towards the site of the tomb. John, the younger man, arrived first; he leaned down and peered into the tomb, but did not go in. He saw the linen clothes that had been used to bind the dead body of Jesus, but nothing else. The Greek word used for 'saw' was '*blepō*' which suggests nothing more than to see.

When Peter arrived, he did not hesitate, but went straight into the tomb, alone. There was no one there. He saw the linen strips that were around Jesus' body, and a little apart from them the square of cloth that had covered His head. This is an important detail showing Peter's attention to what was in the tomb and what was not. Here, the Greek word used for 'saw' was '*theōreō*' which means a careful attention to detail. As a result, we have a detailed description of what he saw inside the tomb. At this point, John joined Peter and we are told he "*saw and believed.*" John, the author, adds the words, "*They still did not understand from Scripture that Jesus had to rise from the dead*" (John 20:9).

As a result of what they saw, they had positive proof that their Master had risen and we are told, "*Then the disciples went back to their homes*" (John 20:10). They had seen with their own eyes proof of what Mary Magdalene had reported. The grave was empty and their Master's body was not there. They had seen all the evidence that was needed that the things Jesus had said had come true, "*that he must go to Jerusalem and suffer many things .... and that he must be killed and on the third day be raised to life*" (Matthew 16:21).

We are told in detail what Peter saw, "*He saw the strips of linen lying there, as well as the burial cloth that had been around Jesus head. The cloth was folded up by itself, separate from the linen*" (John 20:6-7). If the body of Christ had been stolen from the tomb by His friends, it would have been most unlikely that those who stole it would have taken the trouble to remove the linen cloths, fold them up and place them neatly where the body had lain.

Finally, Jesus' words began to make sense. Jesus was going to rise again from the dead. What a wonderful realization it must have been for Peter and John to understand that their Lord and Saviour had risen from the dead. What an important fact for us to know and recognize that Jesus conquered death and because He did, we can have eternal life with Him.

Peter reinstated by Jesus

(John 21:3–19)

Jesus Christ was crucified and God raised Him from the dead. Jesus appeared to His disciples several times during the forty days between His resurrection and ascension. During the time between His second and third appearance, the impulsive Peter decided to return to fishing. Some commentators are of the opinion that Peter had decided to return to his former work of fishing and have nothing more to do with preaching. It seems difficult to understand how a man who lived and worked so closely with the Lord Jesus Christ, and who saw Him in His resurrected body, could forsake his calling to catch men and go back to fishing as his way of life.

Peter said to the other disciples, "*I'm going out to fish*" and they said, "*We'll go with you.*" However, they fished all night and caught nothing. That must have reminded Peter of an incident that took place over three years before, when the Lord had called him from his boat. On that occasion he had also caught nothing, "*Master, we've worked hard all night and haven't caught anything*" (Luke 5:5). Jesus had instructed him to go out and let down his net, which he did, and they caught such a large number of fish that the net was nearly breaking.

Here again in the morning, they were coming near to the shore with an empty net and saw someone standing, but they did not realise that it was Jesus. He asked them, "*Friends, haven't you any fish?*" When they answered "No", He instructed them to throw their net on the other side of the boat and they would catch some. When they obeyed, their catch was so great they were unable to pull in their net.

At this point, John realised it could only be the Master who could do such a miracle and said to Peter, "*It is the Lord!*" As soon as Peter heard this, he wrapped his outer garment around him and jumped into the sea, he was so delighted to see Jesus again and eager to be with the One he had so recently denied. The other disciples followed afterwards in the boat, pulling the net full of fish.

When they landed, they saw that Jesus had a fire burning with several fish on it, and some bread. Jesus asked them to bring some of the fish they had caught and add to what He had on the fire. When they had finished breakfast, Jesus turned to Peter and asked a searching question, "*Simon, son of John, do you truly love me more than these?*" (John 21:15). It is noteworthy that Peter was now standing beside a fire with his Lord and being asked to confess Him publicly, and yet only a few days earlier he was standing beside another fire where he had denied knowing Jesus, the One who had just been arrested (John 18:18, 25).

Some have suggested that Jesus pointed to the boat and net and asked Peter, "*Do you love me more than these?*" You have returned to the fishing but do you love me more than you love fishing?

However, it is more likely that Jesus was referring to the other disciples and challenging Peter about his claim that he would remain loyal to Jesus even if the other disciples deserted Him. Peter had said to Jesus, "*Even if all fall away on account of you, I never will. Even if I have to die with you, I will never disown you*" (Matthew 26:33, 35). Peter was saying how much he loved the Lord, and perhaps suggesting he loved the Lord more than the other disciples. Was Jesus pointing to the other disciples and asking Peter if he still loved Him, even more than the others?

There is also something of interest here that is not apparent in the English language. In the Greek language there are two different words translated into the one word "love". One is *'agape'* and used in John 3:16, where it says, "*For God so loved the world.*" It is also used in Matthew 5:44 "*Love your enemies and pray for those who persecute you.*" It means absolutely unselfish love and is the strongest word for love we have in the Bible. Agape love, in its purest form, requires nothing in return. Having no input from the other person makes it possible for us to love unconditionally. It is used throughout the New Testament for God Himself – "*God is love*" and "*God so loved the world.*"

The other word is *'phileõ'* and suggests a weaker kind of love and is used when speaking of the love or affection such as exists between friends. It is used for family affection and of one friend to another who have common interests and experiences.

It is noteworthy that when the Lord said to Peter, "*Simon, son of John, do you love me more than these?*" He was using *'agape'* for the word 'love', asking Peter if he had unselfish, sacrificial and pure love for Him, over and above what the others had. Peter replied using the other word, saying "*Yes, Lord, you know that I love (phileõ) you*" - You know that I have brotherly love for You. Accepting Peter's acknowledgement that his love was less than Christ had claimed and deserved, Jesus still re-commissioned Peter saying to him, "*Feed my lambs.*" 'Feed' translates a term used of herdsmen pasturing and feeding their livestock. The present tense of the verb denotes continuous action. Jesus described believers as His lambs, emphasizing not only their immaturity, helplessness and need, but also those who are His. Jesus asked Peter to prove the genuineness of his love by feeding His lambs.

Jesus said to Peter again, "*Simon son of John, do you truly love me?*" Again, Jesus used the word '*agape*' but dropped the comparison to '*these others*' and asked a personal question. Peter was still unwilling to claim he possessed the higher sacrificial kind of love. "*Yes, Lord, you know that I love (phileõ) you.*" (You know that I have brotherly love for you). This time in His reply, Jesus said to Peter, "*Take care of my sheep.*" Jesus changed the form of His second question and also the command to Peter. To take care of the sheep expresses the full responsibility that pastoral oversight entails. It is to help them grow and mature, and to know the terrain, the possibility of danger, the presence of predators and the chance of getting lost.

But Jesus was not through with Peter, so He said to him the third time, "*Simon, son of John, do you love (phileõ) Me?*" (Simon son of John, do you have brotherly love for me). Peter was grieved because He said to him the third time, "*Do you love (phileõ) Me?*" (Are you my friend?) Being asked three times by Jesus if he loved Him would remind Peter that he had denied his Master three times and this grieved him. He was also grieved because Jesus changed His vocabulary the third time. Unlike His two previous questions, this third time Jesus used Peter's word for love, *phileo*. Jesus was saying, "*Simon son of John do you have affection for me?*" (Do you only have brotherly love for me?)

This time, Peter pointed out the omniscience of Jesus. He said,

"Lord, you know all things; you know that I love (have affection and brotherly love) you." Jesus said to him, *"Feed, my sheep."* Peter's restoration was now complete. He was commissioned to go and lovingly and tenderly care and nurture the Christians to maturity.

Peter remained obedient to the Lord's commission for the rest of his life. His ministry from that point forward involved not only proclaiming the gospel (Acts 2:14–40; 3:12–26), but also feeding the flock the Lord had entrusted to him (cf. Acts 2:42). Some years later, Peter wrote to the elders of the church, *"Be shepherds of God's flock that is under your care"* (1 Peter 5:2).

Peter continued witnessing for Christ

After writing the Gospel of Luke, Dr. Luke wrote a second book called Acts (Acts of the Apostles), where he continued with an account of the spread of the gospel message after Christ's ascension to heaven.

Luke tells us how Jesus left them, *"and was taken up before their very eyes"* (Acts 1:9). He left them in this way publicly, so that His disciples would not be looking for Him again. After this, they returned to Jerusalem and Peter took on a leadership role among the disciples and led the group (about 120 people) to select an apostle to replace Judas Iscariot. After prayer, Matthias was elected as the new apostle.

When the day of Pentecost came, Peter, along with the other followers of Jesus, was filled with the Holy Spirit (Acts 2). Then Peter stood together with the Eleven and addressed the crowd, explaining the meaning of Jesus' life, death, and resurrection. Peter's leadership in the early church resulted in about 3,000 people being added to their number.

In Acts chapter 3, we again have Peter in prominence. Peter and John went to the temple to pray and they met a man who was lame from birth. Though both disciples are named, it is Peter who says to him, "*Get up and walk.*" With those words the lame man was healed. Following this miracle, Peter again explained the gospel to the crowd that had gathered.

The account of Peter and John being arrested is given in Acts chapter 4. They were taken to a gathering where all the rulers, elders, and scribes of Jerusalem were present, along with Caiaphas the high priest. Peter was again prominent when he proclaimed the message of Jesus and His salvation. Those in charge eventually commanded that Peter and John no longer speak or teach in the name of Jesus, but they refused and finally were released.

In Acts chapter 5, Peter was again in the forefront when Ananias presented an offering to the church, claiming it was all from the sale of a piece of land. Peter discerned that he was lying and deceitful and was misleading the church. As a result Ananias dropped dead at Peter's feet. Three hours later, his wife Sapphira died in a similar manner. Peter's reputation became so great that the sick and possessed were brought to him and many were healed merely with the touch of his shadow (5:15). Later in the chapter, Peter rebuked the council of Pharisees for their lack of belief (5:29) and after a speech from Gamaliel, Peter and John were flogged and then released (5:40).

It is recorded in Acts chapter 8 how Peter and John travelled to Samaria to confirm that the people there accepted the Word of God. A man identified as Simon, who practised sorcery, saw how the believers had received the Holy Spirit after Peter and John placed their hands on them and he wished to obtain this gift, offering the disciples money for it. The account ends with Peter firmly rebuking Simon for making such a request.

In Acts chapter 9, we have an account of Peter at Lydda, healing a man named Aeneas who had been paralysed for eight years. Later in Joppa, Peter learned that a believer named Tabitha (also known by her Greek name, Dorcas) had died. After asking everyone to leave the room, Peter prayed and Tabitha returned to life. This became known all over Joppa and, as a result, many people believed in the Lord Jesus.

In Acts chapter 10, Peter goes to Cornelius' house after receiving a vision from the Lord which removed his prejudiced belief of Gentiles. Peter was invited to be the guest at Cornelius' house. When Peter arrived, he explained that the gospel message of Jesus was important and appropriate to all nations. As Peter was preaching, the Holy Spirit came upon those present in Cornelius' household, including the Gentiles. This was now the third time Peter had been present when the Holy Spirit came upon the believers - in Jerusalem among the Jews, in Samaria among the Samaritans, and in Caesarea among the Gentiles. But when Peter returned to Jerusalem, he was challenged by the "circumcised believers" - Jewish Christians - regarding his visit to the Gentiles. In Acts chapter 11, Peter explained his actions and their doubts were removed, and they praised God that Gentiles were granted repentance unto life and that God had given the Holy Spirit to them.

In Acts chapter 12, we have an account of King Herod (Agrippa I) arresting some believers. Having put James the brother of John to death, and seeing that it pleased the Jews, Herod arrested Peter with the intention of giving him similar treatment after the Passover. However, Peter was miraculously saved by an angel who led him out of prison unharmed. Peter was later able to tell a few believers what happened that night. Following this, Luke says that Peter left for another place (12:17). Luke does not tell us where Peter went but there is the possibility he eventually travelled to Rome, Antioch, Mesopotamia, Corinth, and Edessa.

In Acts chapter 15, we have an account of the Jerusalem Council as it met, to discuss how the Gentiles were to be included among the people of God. After a long debate about requiring the Gentiles to be circumcised and obeying the Law of Moses, Peter delivered a speech which brought the matter to a conclusion. He explained how God had used him to include the Gentiles without any additional burden or requirements. Barnabas and Paul also spoke of the wonderful things God had done among the Gentiles. James, the brother of Jesus, was very supportive of their work and also made the statement that they were not required to be circumcised to join the people of God. Peter's clear declaration of his experience, together with James' explanation of the Hebrew Scriptures, brought a major change in the early church. Peter had a major influence in establishing the Christian faith. There are no further references to Peter in the book of Acts.

When the apostle Paul wrote his letter to the Galatians, he stated that he went up to Jerusalem and stayed with Peter for fifteen days (Galatians 1:18). This was a very important meeting for Paul as Peter, with James and John, were called "pillars" of the church (Galatians 2:9). Paul said that they agreed that he should continue to go to the Gentiles while they go to the Jews (Galatians 2:9).

Peter the author

We have two books in our New Testament attributed to Peter. The first book starts with the words, "*Peter, an apostle of Jesus Christ, to God's elect, strangers in the world scattered throughout Pontus, Galatia, Cappadocia, Asia and Bithynia*" (1 Peter: 1:1). The second book begins with the words, "*Simon Peter, a servant and apostle of Jesus Christ, to those who through the righteousness of our God and Saviour Jesus Christ have received a faith as precious as ours*" (2 Peter 1:1).

Peter reminds his readers that he was an eyewitness of our Lord's sufferings, a fact which we know about from the Gospels. Some have questioned whether Peter, who was an uneducated and ordinary fisherman (Acts 4:13), could produce a letter as well written as this. This query is, however, answered in 1 Peter 5:12, "*With the help of Silas, whom I regard as a faithful brother, I have written to you briefly ...*" Peter used Silas as a scribe to write the letter. The literary form would then, in part, be contributed by Silas. This fact also explains the close resemblances to some of the letters of Paul for whom Silas had rendered the same service. However, Peter was also guided by the Holy Spirit as to what to write.

The first letter was written by Peter towards the end of his life, to give comfort and encouragement to the Christians who were passing through difficult trials and persecution (1 Peter 1:6; 3:9-22; 4:12-19). As Nero's vicious persecution of the Christians started in AD 64, it is generally believed that Peter wrote prior to that, perhaps AD 63. Paul was martyred about AD 64 and Peter was to lose his life shortly afterwards.

The only clue as to where Peter was when he wrote the letter is found in 1 Peter 5:13, suggesting it was written "in Babylon," where a Christian church had been established. Babylon was the most famous city in Mesopotamia, whose ruins lie in modern-day Iraq, 59 miles south west of Bagdad. It was a commercial, administrative, literary, and religious centre of pure, uncompromising Judaism. Acts 2:9 tells us that Jews from this area were present, with many from other countries, on the day of Pentecost.

Babylon was beyond the eastern frontier of the Roman Empire while Rome, at its centre, was far to the west. Babylon was where Peter apparently had a ministry among the many Jews scattered there from previous centuries. He was there preaching that the Messiah had come, that Jesus Christ was that promised Messiah, and that Jesus Christ was the only hope of salvation.

Peter wrote this letter to encourage the scattered Christians, who were bewildered, because they were being persecuted. He did this by stressing that God's grace gave hope to the Christian. This hope far surpassed any suffering they may have to bear. He also stressed that the best preparation for suffering was to have the same attitude as Christ (1 Peter 4:1). This was expanded throughout the whole letter in terms of practical holiness. To walk in humble submission to God was the only satisfactory state of life in which to meet the attacks of the devil (5:6ff). Peter gave them practical guidance as to how they should react, even when their suffering was not deserved, and urged them to stand firm (3:13-17). The advice was based upon Peter's teaching about the nature of their salvation and the example set by their Saviour.

The second Epistle of Peter has long been the subject of much discussion about its authorship. When 2 Peter was compared with 1 Peter, it was noticed that the writer used a very different style from that of 1 Peter. This made some think it might not have been written by Peter. Also in 2 Peter 3:15-16 Peter refers to Paul's letters as scripture. Many scholars argue that there was no collection of Paul's letters in Peter's time and that no one had yet formed the opinion that Paul's writings were scripture. But we must take note of the fact that 2 Peter 3:15 does not expressly refer to a collection of Paul's letters, nor do we have to see that there is a reference to all the letters Paul wrote. Peter simply refers to those of Paul's letters with which he was acquainted. We may ask who would be better equipped to recognise Paul's writings as scripture than Peter, a fellow apostle.

We know that the writer of this letter was an apostle (2 Peter 3:2). He was one of the privileged three on the Mount of Transfiguration (1:18). Also, that he had written a letter prior to this letter to the same people (3:1) and therefore the claim of 1 Peter 1:1 is the only logical possibility.

In this second letter, Peter was not facing so much the outward dangers of persecution, but the more subtle inward danger of false teaching and a heresy causing men even to deny "*the sovereign Lord who bought them*" (2 Peter 2:1). In chapter 2, he has written of what will happen and warned his readers against yielding to the subtle temptations which he reckoned would surely come to them. One of the marked features of the letter is its emphasis on "knowing our Lord." The perils of apostasy are shown in terms of a departure from such knowledge (2:20ff). The first letter was written to console, the second to warn; in the first, we have much about suffering, in the second, much about error.

Peter's final years

The New Testament is silent on Peter's general whereabouts, following his escape from prison, after being arrested by King Herod (Agrippa 1) in the early 40s AD (Acts 12). After this, Paul became the major personality, with Peter only briefly reappearing when attending the Council at Jerusalem several years later (approximately AD 49). He attended the conference of the apostles and other church leaders, as Luke records in Acts 15. Afterwards, the New Testament record says nothing about where Peter was working, except for one comment in his own letter of 1 Peter 5:13, when he passed on greetings from church members in Babylon.

The apostle Paul wrote, "*On the contrary, they saw I had been given the task of preaching the gospel to the Gentiles, just as Peter had been given the task of preaching the gospel to the Jews. For God, who was at work in the ministry of Peter as an apostle to the Jews, was also at work in my ministry as an apostle to the Gentiles. James, Peter and John, those reputed to be pillars, gave me and Barnabas the right hand of fellowship when they recognised the grace given to me. They agreed that we should go to the Gentiles, and they to the Jews*" (Galatians 2:7-9).

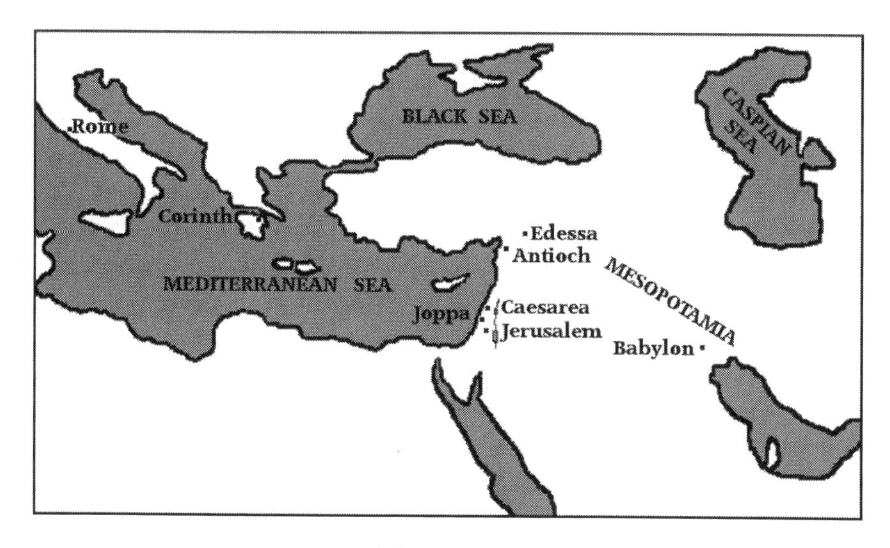

Map of places Peter visited

The question is often asked, was the apostle Peter ever in the City of Rome during his ministry? Peter was preaching to the people of Babylon when he wrote the letters of 1 and 2 Peter. He wrote to those who were in Asia Minor, comprising most of what is present day Turkey. All of the districts mentioned in 1 Peter 1:1 are in a little section of eastern Turkey. The New Testament gives no statement or hint that Peter was ever in the City of Rome, the Capital of the Roman Empire in his day.

In fact, it is significant that the apostle Paul, when writing his letters, did not mention that the apostle Peter had been in Rome. Paul wrote much of the New Testament that covers many years, several missionary tours and the founding of many churches. He wrote to the church in Rome and he also wrote several letters from Rome and mentions Christians by name in each of them, but he never referred to Peter.

In the last chapter of the book of Romans, Paul sent greetings to twenty-seven members of the church, members of the body of Christ, the saints in Rome, but he did not mention Peter whom he knew. There is also no mention of Peter in Rome during Paul's two-year stay there in Acts 28, about AD 60-62.

There are those who teach Peter was there from AD 42 to 67 and was the head of the church; if that was the case, he had been in Rome for about sixteen years when Paul wrote the book of Romans around AD 58. It would be strange that Paul should send greetings to twenty-seven church members and did not say a word of greeting to the pastor of the church.

Surely the reason Paul did not mention Peter was because he was not there at that time, and was not the founder of the church in Rome. If Peter had founded the church in Rome, it is unlikely that Paul would have gone there, for his policy was to work where other Apostles had not laboured (Romans 15:18-22).

Peter nowhere claimed superiority over the other apostles. In his writings (1 and 2 Peter) he does not claim any special role, authority, or power over the church. Nowhere in Scripture does Peter, or any other apostle, state that their apostolic authority would be passed on to successors. It is true the Apostle Peter had a leadership role among the disciples and played a crucial role in the early spread of the gospel (Acts chapters 1-10). Peter was the "rock" that Christ predicted he would be (Matthew 16:18). However, these truths about Peter in no way give support to the concept that Peter was the first Bishop of Rome, or that he was the "supreme leader" over the apostles, or that his authority would be passed on to the successive bishops of Rome. Peter himself points us all to the true Shepherd and Overseer of the church, the Lord Jesus Christ (1 Peter 2:25).

Scripture does not record how Peter died. We know that Jesus seemed to indicate that Peter would die as a martyr, "*You will stretch out your hands, and someone else will dress you and lead you where you do not want to go*" (John 21:18-19). There is a tradition that Peter died in Rome by means of crucifixion, (with arms outstretched) at the time of the Great Fire of Rome in the year AD 64. Prior to that, he had been taken as a prisoner and condemned to the Mamertine prison in Rome. It was a most horrible and brutal prison of barbaric inhumanity where light never entered and the stench and filth was intolerable.

It is traditionally held that he was crucified upside down at his own request, since he saw himself unworthy to be crucified in the same way as Jesus Christ. This took place three months after the disastrous fire that destroyed Rome for which the emperor Nero blamed the Christians.

PHILIP
THE CAUTIOUS ONE

Philip is the fifth name in every list of the twelve apostles in the four Gospels. Philip is a Greek name meaning "lover of horses." It has been suggested that Philip was called after Philip II of Macedon. His son, Alexander the Great, at the age of thirty, was the creator of one of the largest empires in ancient history, leaving behind a lasting Greek influence. Many people in the Middle East then accepted the Greek customs, culture and language. They were known as "Hellenists." It is possible that Philip came from a family of Hellenistic Jews. Philip was a Jew, but the Greek influence in his life proved to be valuable in his future ministry.

Another suggestion was that Philip was named in honour of Philip the Tetrarch (34-4 BC), son of Herod the Great, who inherited the north east part of his father's kingdom. He had honoured the town of Bethsaida, where Philip was born, by granting it the status of a city. Andrew and Peter also came from the town of Bethsaida (John 1:44).

Philip the Apostle should not be confused with Philip the deacon. The early church chose seven men to care for the widows who "*were being overlooked in the daily distribution of food*" (Acts 6:1). Philip the deacon was chosen as one of those seven men with Stephen, the first martyr. This Philip was the one who witnessed to the Ethiopian eunuch after reading from the prophet Isaiah, as he travelled in his chariot on the road from Jerusalem to Gaza (Acts 8:26-40).

Philip's Call

(John 1:43)

In John 1:35-42 we have the account of Andrew and John following Jesus after they had seen John the Baptist point to Jesus and say, '*Look, the lamb of God!*' After that experience, Andrew looked for his brother Simon and told him '*We have found the Messiah*' and brought him to Jesus. Andrew and John had followed Jesus as a result of the testimony of John the Baptist, and Simon had been brought to Jesus by his brother Andrew.

We are then told, "*The next day Jesus decided to leave for Galilee. Finding Philip, He said to him, 'Follow me'*" (John1:43). Philip was the first person Jesus Himself called directly to follow Him, though in fact, all the disciples were chosen before the foundation of the world. Jesus told them, "*You did not choose me, but I chose you to go and bear fruit*" (John 15:16).

All true Christians have been called and chosen by God, but not every believer has the same experience in coming to faith in Jesus Christ. We must not expect the experience of others to be the same as our own, because the Holy Spirit is sovereign and unique in every life.

Philip was seeking after God

It is worth noting that Philip had been seeking after God for he told Nathanael, "*We have found the one Moses wrote about in the Law, and about whom the prophets also wrote*" (John 1:45). Clearly, Philip had been studying the Law and the Prophets to find information about the Messiah. Here is evidence of a seeking heart finding a seeking Saviour.

Note that Jesus found Philip. The Good Shepherd went after the sheep. What was true here is equally true in every genuine conversion. Our seeking of Him is the reflex action of His first seeking us. So it is with each believer, for we learn from Luke 19:10 that the Lord Jesus "*... is come to seek and to save that which was lost.*"

Philip was right in what he told Nathanael about the Lord Jesus, but he had yet to learn what Jesus said, "*no-one can come to me unless the Father who sent me draws him*" (John 6:44). It was not Philip who 'found' the Lord Jesus, rather the Lord Jesus who 'found' Philip.

Here, we have a perfect illustration of sovereign election and human choice working together. Philip felt he had found the Lord and yet God is the One who seeks and finds. Scripture says, "*Seek and you will find*" (Matthew 7:7); "*Seek the Lord while he may be found*" (Isaiah 55:6), but it also says, "*For the Son of Man came to seek and to save what was lost*" (Luke 19:10); "*We have been chosen according to the foreknowledge of God the Father*" (1 Peter 1:2).

We are told that when Jesus called Philip he followed immediately. He was quickly convinced that Jesus was the fulfilment of the law and prophets - He was the Messiah.

The Importance of the Old Testament Scriptures

We must also note how the Old Testament clearly teaches about Christ. He was the one promised when Adam and Eve sinned in the Garden of Eden; He was the One promised in the days of Moses, Noah, Abraham, Isaac and Jacob. He was the one who was "*pierced for our transgressions, he was crushed for our iniquities .. and by his wounds we are healed*" (Isaiah 53:5). He was the One foretold by many of the Prophets including Isaiah, Jeremiah, Ezekiel and Malachi.

We should not neglect reading and studying the Old Testament claiming that it tells us nothing about Jesus Christ. Christ is there and we should diligently search to find Him.

Philip Witnesses to Nathanael

(John 1:45-46)

No sooner had Philip found the seeking Saviour than he wanted to share his discovery with his friend Nathanael. John writes, "*Philip found Nathanael and told him, 'We have found the One Moses wrote about in the Law, and about whom the prophets also wrote – Jesus of Nazareth, the son of Joseph'*" (John 1:45). Obviously excited at having met the promised Messiah, and by faith believing in Him, Philip immediately seeks to tell Nathanael of the one 'he found'.

Philip describes our Lord as "*Jesus of Nazareth, the son of Joseph.*" Later in John's Gospel, we read how the Jews were arguing as to who Jesus was, and they said, "*Is this not Jesus, the son of Joseph, whose father and mother we know? How can he now say,*

'I came down from heaven'?" (John 6:42). The statement "Son of Joseph" shows the belief that the Jews had about our Lord's birth. They believed Him to be the natural son of Joseph, the husband of Mary. Jesus was simply known as the son of Joseph, the carpenter.

The announcement by the angel Gabriel to Mary that she was to have a child miraculously conceived by the power of the Holy Spirit was apparently a matter of which the Jews had no knowledge until after the death of the Virgin Mary and all her family (Luke 1:26-38).

Philip was convinced that Jesus was the fulfilment of the Law and prophets. However, it was when he expressed his conviction to Nathanael that he ran into a problem. Nathanael asked, *"Can any good thing come out of Nazareth?"* (John 1:46).

Philip could have entered into a discussion with him about how Jesus was the fulfilment of the Old Testament prophets. Philip refused to argue but simply answered, "Come and see" (v. 46). Discussion and argument may lay a good foundation for faith but we cannot argue anyone into the kingdom of God.

If Philip had criticized Nathanael for his unbelief, he might have caused him to turn and go away; if he had debated and discussed with him about Jesus coming from Nazareth, he might have failed to convince him and possibly even increased his doubts. Inviting him to come and meet Jesus and determine for himself who He was, proved to be the right choice. We should never be afraid or ashamed to deal with people the way Philip dealt with Nathanael. Let us confidently invite them to bring their doubts and fears to Jesus.

Invite Others to see Jesus

If a person feels unable to witness about Jesus Christ or enter into a discussion about spiritual matters, it is a wise decision to trust Jesus Christ with the situation. It could be said, *"I'm not able to answer all your questions, but I can introduce you to someone who has the answers."* Philip's strategy paid off. Because of his encounter with Jesus, Nathanael was convinced of Jesus' Messiahship.

Today so few people are willing, or have the desire, to invite others to come to Christ. It has often been the case that the one who does the most good for souls, is the one who speaks personally to an individual and invites that person to "come and see" the one who has changed their own life. Philip has set us an example in the success and importance of that personal invitation.

A passion for souls is rare among church members today. The majority of those who profess the name of Jesus feel little responsibility for the souls of others. If we spent more time with the Master then we would have that burning desire to invite others to meet Him. Let us not forget, "*For God so loved the world that he gave his one and only Son, that whoever believes in him shall not perish but have eternal life*" (John 3:16).

The Feeding of the Five Thousand

(John 6:5-7)

The next time we meet Philip is at the feeding of the five thousand. Jesus had crossed over to the other side of the Sea of Galilee with His disciples and sat down with them on the hillside. However, a great crowd of people followed Him, for they had seen the miracles He had performed on the sick and wanted to see more.

When Jesus saw the crowd coming, He knew they would soon be hungry and said to Philip, "*Where shall we buy bread for these people to eat?*" (John 6:5). Why did Jesus single out Philip by asking this question when it was Judas who was in charge of the money? John tells us that Jesus asked Philip this question to test him for He already knew what He was going to do.

Philip had been with Jesus since the beginning of His ministry and had seen many miracles, would he now pass the test and say, 'Lord that is no problem for You, You can feed them without any difficulty by one of your miracles.' Sadly Philip failed the test!

Perhaps Philip was asked because he came from Bethsaida which was near to the place where they were. He would therefore have a fairly good idea where provisions could be bought. Alternatively, he may have been a practical man and could have been the one responsible for organising the provisions for Jesus and the disciples, and was therefore asked where he was going to get food for everyone on that occasion.

While thinking about this, Philip started to count up what it would cost and came to the conclusion that it would require over 200 denarii worth of bread. This absolute minimum would give everyone just a little, since a denarius was a workman's pay for one day. So Philip, the cautious man that he was, says, "*Eight months wages would not buy enough bread for each one to have a bite*" (John 6:6).

Philip's Faith was Tested

This whole event was to test Philip's faith to see whether he believed that Jesus was God and the God who provides. This, however, was not an unfair test for Philip, as he was present when

Jesus turned water into wine in Cana (John 2:1-11); he was with Jesus when He healed the dying son of the Royal Official without going to his home (John 4:43-54), and he saw Jesus heal the invalid at the pool of Bethesda (John 5:1-8). So, Philip's faith should have demonstrated the belief that Jesus was God and could do all things.

Philip, however, was not getting the purpose of these signs which was to show that Jesus was God incarnate. In fact, later, Philip would say to Jesus, "*Lord, show us the Father and that will be enough for us*" (John 14:8). Jesus replied, "*Don't you know me, Philip, even after I have been among you such a long time? Anyone who has seen me has seen the Father. How can you say, 'Show us the Father'?*" (John 14:9).

Jesus knew the heart of Philip. He was eager to follow Jesus when he was called, without any doubts and most likely with a lot of zeal. This zeal led him to witness to Nathanael who had doubts about Jesus coming from Nazareth. In spite of his enthusiasm, Jesus knew that Philip was lacking the depth of faith He was looking for in the future evangelist. When Jesus tested Philip's faith by asking him the question, "Where shall we buy bread for these people to eat?" he failed.

In effect, Philip considered it impossible to feed the people in that place. Philip portrayed the situation as hopeless, unrealistic, and not feasible. In doing so, Philip failed the definition of faith as given by Hebrews 11:1, "*Now faith is being sure of what we hope for and certain of what we do not see.*"

Philip was a man of limited vision. Depending solely on proofs and calculations, he forgot the Lord was ready to meet any emergency. Philip never thought of divine power to feed the thousands; to him it was a matter of money. His temperament ruled out the miraculous. He did not bring God into the picture.

Is that not the problem many of us face daily? We meet the unexpected situation and try to resolve it by our own way, failing to bring the God of miracles into the situation.

Do we believe that Jesus has the power to multiply resources and the power over anything in this world? Do we believe that Jesus can solve the impossible and can change a hopeless situation into one with hope? When Jesus is involved, we must accept as real what may appear to be unrealistic or unworkable.

Philip was Taught a Lesson

To help Philip in the school of faith, Jesus asked him about bread for the crowd. When Philip gave his answer, Jesus turned to Andrew who was standing with a boy holding his lunch. Philip's negative attitude not only lacked faith but may have affected Andrew, because when he brought the boy with his lunch he said, "*Here is a boy with five small barley loaves and two small fish, but how far will they go among so many?*" (John 6:9).

Was Andrew's faith also showing signs of doubt? The lesson to be learned is that if we keep company with doubting people, it can cause us also to have doubts. Perhaps Andrew had the faint hope and faith that Jesus could rescue this situation in some way.

However, in response to Andrew's statement, Jesus requested the people to sit down. After giving thanks, He distributed the bread and fish to the crowd, multiplying the boy's lunch sufficiently to feed the whole crowd, and with what was left over, filling twelve baskets. Philip must have stared at Jesus in wonder and amazement. Philip learned that day that little is much if God is in it, and he would have wanted to include God when making important decisions in the future.

The church needs cautious and wise leaders to safeguard against extravagant money spending ideas. However, in contrast, the church also needs men and women of faith to see greater things being accomplished with God's help. Philip needed to exchange his thoughts of the impossible for the possible through God.

Too often, when in a difficult situation, we fail to consider what God can do. When the Israelites came to the Red Sea, hemmed in and pursued by the Egyptians, their situation looked impossible: *"but God"* parted the waters to bring them safely through (Exodus 14:8-31). When Peter was in prison awaiting execution in the morning, it seemed everything was over for him. *"But God"* released his chains and opened the prison gate to free him (Acts 12:1-10). Paul reminds us that at one time we were gratifying the cravings of our sinful nature and were objects of God's wrath. *"But God,"* because of His great love for us, made us alive with Christ even when we were dead in transgressions (Ephesians 2:3-5).

Situations and circumstances may look impossible for us, *"but God"* is able. The Lord must be taken into consideration. Jesus saw the need of this crowd and knew what He was going to do about it. Perhaps you are a believer finding yourself in a difficult situation and wondering if God has forgotten about you, then be assured He knows all about it. He is not going to let you down, He is not going to leave you nor forsake you. It may seem as though there is no possible way of meeting your present need, but He knows what He will do. We look at situations from a human point of view, *"but God"* can do the impossible – do you believe that?

The question was, "*Where shall we buy bread for these people to eat*?" Andrew produced five small barley loaves and two small fish. Over five thousand people were fed and twelve baskets were collected of the pieces left over. God does not do things in a miserly way – He always gives more than is needed. Do not be afraid to include Jesus in the challenging situations you find yourself. "*My God will meet all your needs according to His glorious riches in Christ Jesus*" (Philippians 4:19).

The Greeks asked Philip for Help to Meet Jesus
(John 12:20-22)

The next encounter with Philip was when some Greeks came to worship at the Feast of the Passover. They came to Philip and asked, "*Sir, we would like to see Jesus*" (v.21).

These Greeks were either God-fearing Gentiles or full proselytes of Judaism who were coming to Jerusalem to worship God at the Passover. This event happened after Jesus' triumphal entry into Jerusalem, so there was great excitement and debate going around Jerusalem as to who He was. Could this have caused these Greeks to have a desire to meet Jesus? Had they come to Jerusalem for the Passover with the desire of knowing more about the Christ they had heard so much about?

Matthew records that, after Jesus' triumphant entry into Jerusalem, He entered the temple area and drove out all who were buying and selling (Matthew 21:12). Since this was in the 'outer court,' often called 'the court of the Gentiles,' it may well be that these Greeks had been in this area, and saw what happened and requested to see Jesus.

The Gentiles were only able to go to the outer court and not allowed to go any further into the Temple. These courts were separated by a low wall. Josephus, the Jewish historian of the first century AD, wrote about the warning signs in Greek and Latin that were placed on the barrier wall that separated the court of the Gentiles from the other courts in the temple.

Strangers were warned of the death penalty for anyone who should pass from the outer court into that of the Jews. There can be no doubt that the wall was one of those boundaries which separated the Jews from the Gentiles, of which Josephus speaks. Non-Jews were not permitted to enter the temple area. The outer court derived its name from the fact that Gentiles were permitted into this area provided they conducted themselves in a reverent and respectful manner.

The Greeks Came to Philip

Why did these Greeks come to Philip? Was it because he bore a Greek name and perhaps they thought he also was a Greek and could speak Greek? Were they acquainted with him previously? Was Philip the organiser of events (remember Jesus asked Philip how he proposed to feed the five thousand) and so they came to him to arrange a meeting with Jesus?

Philip did not act immediately but hesitated while he consulted Andrew. Perhaps he was not sure what to do and how Jesus would respond to the request. Jesus had earlier given instructions to His disciples when He had sent them out, "*Do not go among the Gentiles or enter any town of the Samaritans. Go rather to the lost sheep of Israel*" (Matthew 10:5-6). On another occasion Jesus told His disciples, after a Canaanite woman came to Him to heal her demon-possessed daughter, "*I was sent only to the lost sheep of Israel*" (Matthew 15:24). Jesus had told the Samaritan woman, "*Salvation is from the Jews*" (John 4:22).

On the other hand, Jesus had healed the Canaanite woman's daughter. We are also told that many Samaritans believed that Jesus was "*the Saviour of the world,*" after He had revealed to the woman at the well that He was the Messiah and had preached to the people of the town (John 4:42). Therefore, the problem that Philip had was that these Greeks were not Jews – they were aliens, foreigners, Gentiles, one step below the Samaritans – would Jesus want to meet them?

It is clear, however, that Jesus was not racist towards non-Jews but rather He felt an obligation to proclaim the coming of His kingdom first to Israel in fulfilment of the Old Testament prophets. Paul said, "*I am not ashamed of the gospel, because it is the power of God for the salvation of everyone who believes: first for the Jew, then for the Gentile*" (Romans 1:16).

John said, "*He came to that which was his own, but his own did not receive Him. Yet to all who received him, to those who believed in his name, he gave the right to become children of God*" (John 1:11-12). Jesus left heaven and came to earth to be the Saviour of the world. Anyone who believes in Him will have their sins forgiven, and will enter eternal life.

When Philip discussed the situation with Andrew, he did not hesitate; he and Philip went to tell Jesus that the Greeks wanted to see Him. Some commentators are sure Jesus met with the Greeks and preached the gospel to them.

The Coming of the Greeks was a Sign

It would appear that Jesus looked upon the coming of the Greeks as a sign that He had reached the climax of His mission, for John tells us what Jesus replied. He said, "*The hour has come for the son of Man to be glorified. I tell you the truth, unless an ear of wheat falls to the ground and dies, it remains only a single seed. But if it dies, it produces many seeds. The man who loves his life will lose it, while the man who hates his life in this world will keep it for eternal life. Whoever serves me must follow me; and where I am, my servant also will be. My Father will honour the one who serves me ....*" (John 12:23-36).

For Jesus to say "*The hour has come....*" is clearly a change from His previous statements. In John 2:1-11, we have the account of Jesus changing water into wine. Jesus' mother had said to Him, "*They have no more wine*" and Jesus' reply to her was "*My time has not yet come.*"

In John 7:1-13, we have the account of Jesus' brothers wanting Him to go to Judea and perform miracles so that people might believe in Him - that He should become public (although his own brothers did not believe in him at this time). Jesus' reply was, "*The time for me has not yet come.*"

Then in John 7:25-43, we have the account of Jesus teaching in the temple court and the crowd had tried to seize Him but no one laid a hand on Him, and John said, "*because his time had not yet come*" (v.30).

In John 8:12-29, we have another account of Jesus speaking to the people that He was the light of the world and how the Pharisees challenged Him. Later they tried to arrest Him, "*Yet no-one seized him, because his time had not yet come*" (v.20).

All throughout the three years of his public ministry this had been the situation, but then it changed and Jesus said, "*The hour has come for the Son of Man to be glorified.*" Later John tells us how Jesus washed His disciples' feet in the upper room because He "*knew that the time had come for him to leave this world and go to the Father*" (John 13:1). Then, in the Garden of Gethsemane, He prayed: "*Father, the time has come. Glorify your Son that your Son may glorify You*" (John 17:1).

The Greeks, who wanted to meet Jesus, believed in God, and

obviously understood Jewish custom and scripture and practised the Jewish faith - they were not pagans. Yet, unlike most of the Jewish people with whom they worshipped, they recognized Jesus as the Messiah and wanted to meet Him.

Jesus came to save the Hebrew nation, and most of them rejected Him, but the non-Jews came to Him. Thus, Jesus marks the occasion as an indication of the end of His earthly ministry and the time of His return to heaven in a glorified form.

Jesus was about to be rejected by His own people, but the scriptures had said that, if Israel rejected Him, He should become a light for revelation to the Gentiles. So here is the first evidence of this being fulfilled when these Greeks made their request, "*We want to see Jesus.*"

Despite the restrictions on the Gentiles entering the temple, these God-fearing Greeks wanted to see Jesus. It is interesting that they sought to see Jesus at the very time when the Jews sought to kill Him. In Luke 23:8 we read of another man, Herod Antipas, who also strongly desired to see Jesus, but Herod's motives were different from those of the Greeks. Herod wanted to see Jesus perform some miracles so that he, Herod Antipas, could be entertained.

The Importance of Seeing Jesus

John the Baptist was the first person mentioned in John's Gospel who saw Jesus and immediately recognised Him as the Lamb of God – the promised Messiah (John 1:29). Then Andrew left John the Baptist and began to follow Jesus. He asked Jesus where He was staying and Jesus replied with the simple invitation: "*Come and see.*"

Just a few verses later, Philip, having already seen Jesus for himself, invited Nathanael to "*come and see*" Jesus (John 1:45-46). Nathanael wondered if anything good could come from a place like Nazareth. Because of what he saw, Nathanael confessed that Jesus is the Son of God, to which Jesus replied, "*You will see greater things than these.*" Nicodemus also wanted to see Jesus, having already recognised Him to be a teacher sent from God (John 3:1-2).

Jesus had changed people's lives and on this occasion it was no different. This time it was "*some Greeks*" [that is, some Gentiles] who wanted to meet Jesus.

Only Jesus can save people from their sins. Salvation is found in no one but Jesus, the eternal Son of God, the sinless Lamb of God. Jesus *is the Messiah.* He made this profound statement to the sinful Samaritan woman in John 4:26. He said to her, "*I who speak to you am he,*" meaning, "I am the Messiah." There is no other Messiah, no other Saviour, and no other Deliverer. That is why we ought to say, "*Sir, we would like to see Jesus.*"

Jesus *is the Son of God.* We find this reference to Jesus throughout the gospel accounts as well as the rest of the New Testament. What an amazing revelation. Jesus "*is the way, the truth, and the life.*" He is the only way to the Father.

What about you? Do you want to see Jesus? If you have a personal encounter with Him, your life will be transformed.

Philip asks to see the Father

(John 14:1-14)

Jesus talked to the disciples about heaven and how He would soon be leaving them. Jesus' heart was heavy as He knew what lay ahead for Him the next day, and that His time with the disciples was almost finished. He was going to send the Holy Spirit to give them power to be His witnesses. They would face a hostile, Christ-rejecting world, and He warned them, "*I am sending you out like sheep among wolves*" (Matthew 10:16).

He urged them not to be troubled in their hearts for He was going to prepare a place for them. They would be left alone by Him on earth but one day they would be with Him in heaven for ever.

One of the reasons why our Lord went away was to get ready a dwelling-place for His disciples. Heaven is a prepared place for a prepared people to be with Him forever and this is a comforting thought for the Christian.

Thomas said, "*Lord we don't know where you are going, so how can we know the way*" (John 14:5). Jesus had just explained that He was going to prepare a place for them, but their concern was how they were going to get to this place as they did not know where it was.

Jesus Reveals who He is to Philip

Jesus then explained, "*I am the way and the truth and the life. No-one comes to the Father except through me.*" Jesus was going to the Father in heaven, and the only way for them to get there was through faith in Christ. No one can go to heaven without Christ, He is the only way; there is no other way in spite of what many people may say or believe.

In John 14:6-7, Jesus made an amazing claim about Himself. He not only said that He was the way to God, the truth about God and the very life of God but He said He was God. He told them, "*If you really knew me, you would know my Father as well.*" Jesus was clearly stating that He was God – to know Christ was to know the Father. To see Him was to see the Father.

Philip listened to what Jesus said to Thomas and, not knowing what He meant, said, "*Lord show us the Father and that will be enough for us*" (John 14:8). Philip wanted some outward and visible manifestation of God. God had appeared in various ways to the prophets and saints of old and Philip affirmed that, if some such manifestation should be made to them, they would be satisfied.

It was right to want evidence that Jesus was the Messiah, but such evidence had been shown repeatedly in the miracles and teaching of Jesus, and that should have been enough for them. Jesus told Philip, "*Don't you know me Philip, even after I have been among you such a long time*?" Philip had been with Jesus since the beginning of His ministry, three years earlier.

Jesus had raised the dead, cast out devils and healed the sick which no one could have done who had not come from God. In that time, they had every opportunity to learn His character and His mission from God. Therefore, it was not necessary, after so many proofs of His divine mission, that God should visibly manifest Himself to them in order that they might be convinced that Jesus came from Him.

Philip had heard His words, seen His works and still there was a sad lack of understanding. He did not know the Father. Yet every word and work of Jesus Christ was in perfect, divine harmony with the Father's will. The Lord Jesus, in every act, revealed the Father to the Jews. Even the apostles, whom He had called, seemed to have missed this amazing revelation – to see Jesus, to watch Him, to hear Him, to see His miracles and tender loving compassion which was indeed to see the full expression of the Father revealed. All that could be known of the Father has been perfectly revealed in Jesus Christ.

Philip's Knowledge was Incomplete

Philip, like the other disciples, was a man of incomplete knowledge and understanding of who Jesus was and how little he realised that Jesus and His Father were one. His faith was weak and he wanted proof of everything before he would believe. In fact, Jesus gives Philip a gentle rebuke by reminding him that he had been "*such a long time*" with Him and still did not seem to understand who He was.

Jesus goes even further in His rebuke to Philip by saying, "*Don't you believe that I am in the Father, and the Father is in me? The words I say to you are not just my own. Rather, it is the Father, living in me, who is doing his work*" (John 14:10). Everything that Jesus did as man here in this world, He did in fellowship and agreement with the Father. That is why He could say that the Son could do nothing of Himself as everything was in harmony with the will of the Father.

We are certainly indebted to Philip for his question, as Jesus' answer contains the central declaration of the Christian faith, namely that Jesus is God. In Jesus, God is at work. In Jesus, God's plans for His children are revealed.

Philip's final days

Only a few days after Philip made the request to see the Father, Jesus was judged, flogged and crucified. While we do not know all the details about what happened to Philip, we have enough to convince us that he, along with the other apostles, went forth to proclaim the unsearchable riches of Christ.

He appears in the list of those present in the Upper Room (Acts 1:13), where they all joined together in prayer, and where Matthias was chosen to replace Judas Iscariot. He was present when they were all filled with the Holy Spirit as Jesus had promised and they spoke in other languages (Acts 2:1-7).

Following the martyrdom of Stephen, the church in Jerusalem was severely persecuted. Prominent in leading the persecution was young Saul, going so far as entering homes and dragging men and women off to prison (Acts 8:3).

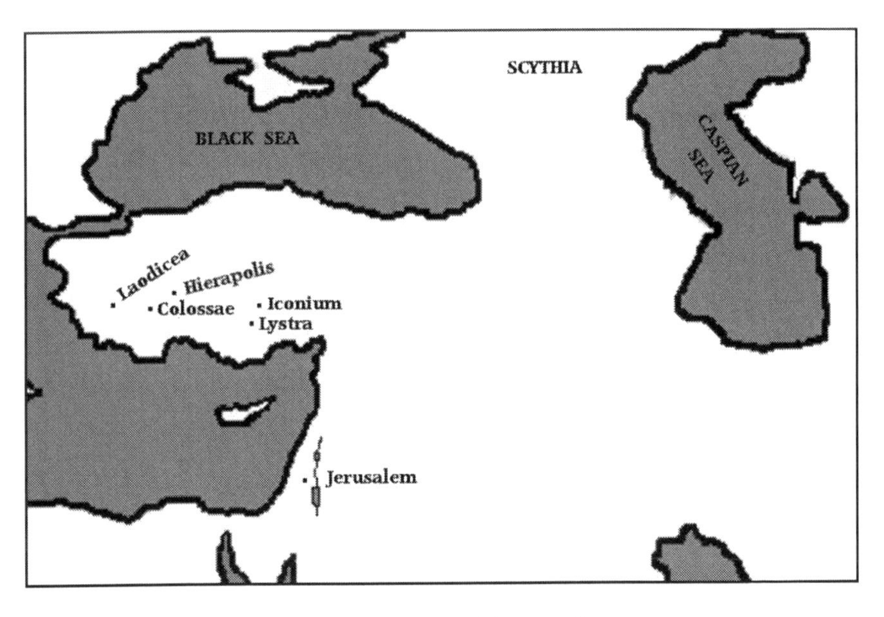

Map of places Philip visited

This led to the dispersion of the church throughout Judea and Samaria, though the apostles remained in Jerusalem. Those who were scattered went everywhere preaching the Word and performing miracles; many Samaritans believed and were baptised, including a sorcerer named Simon. When the apostles in Jerusalem heard that the Samaritans had received the Word, they sent Peter and John to them. They prayed for them that they might receive the Holy Spirit through the laying on of hands (Acts 8:14-17).

It is believed that Philip travelled into Scythia (south Russia) and remained there preaching the Gospel for twenty years; he then preached at Hierapolis in Phrygia (Upper Asia). Hierapolis was the ancient Roman-Greek city on top of hot springs located in south western Turkey, near Denizli. Philip was ideally suited for a ministry to Greek-speaking people after the experience he had with the Greek people wanting to see Jesus.

From the second century BC, the hot springs at Hierapolis had been used as a spa where sick people came, believing it helped their various ailments. In the first century it was part of the area of Laodicea, Colossae and Hierapolis. Paul refers to the two cities of Hierapolis and Laodicea in his epistle to the Colossians (Colossians 4:13). By the time John wrote the book of the Revelation, the church at Laodicea was singled out for attention (Revelation 3:14-22). There is a tradition, although not certain, that Philip travelled from Hierapolis to preach in France.

Philip Faithful to the End

It is believed that Philip was martyred in the city of Hierapolis, his death occurring in AD 80, during the reign of the Roman Emperor Titus. There is also a tradition that he died in AD 90, during the persecutions of Domitian. Philip's preaching, and the subsequent conversion to Christianity of the wife of the Roman Proconsul, enraged the Proconsul who had Philip and Bartholomew, who were working together, tortured and sentenced to death.

Philip and Bartholomew were then crucified (the Greeks say

head downwards) and Philip preached from his cross. As a result of Philip's preaching, the crowd released Bartholomew, but Philip insisted that they do not release him, and he died on the cross.

Philip was a man for whom, in the early days, faith was difficult. However, this cautious and slow of learning apostle, took his questions to Jesus and his faith grew.

We are indebted to Philip for some of those questions, as Jesus' answers contain valuable truths that Jesus is God. In Jesus, God is at work; in Jesus, God's plans for His children are revealed; to follow Jesus' example is to walk in God's way.

When we are demanding proof, it is Jesus Christ who supplies the practical, down-to-earth answers. The Lord wants us to look beyond our own limited resources to His infinite power and presence. Therefore, what we need today is to have a closer walk with God. Maybe we are reluctant to share Jesus with others in the district where we live, or with a different culture or faith. Let us learn from Philip the lesson he learned with the Greeks wanting to see Jesus, and later in life as he ministered to the Greeks and saw many coming to faith in Christ.

NATHANAEL BARTHOLOMEW

NOTHING FALSE

The name Nathanael appears only in John's Gospel and the name Bartholomew is never mentioned; whereas the name Bartholomew occurs in the list of Christ's apostles recorded in the other three gospels (Matthew 10:3; Mark 3:18; Luke 6:14). Since Nathanael and Bartholomew are both included in the list of the twelve disciples.but never appear together, it is believed the names refer to the same person.

These names are also both linked to the apostle Philip, giving further evidence that they are the same person. Bartholomew and Philip appear together in the list of the twelve disciples mentioned in the first three Gospels and in Acts. In John's gospel Nathanael and Philip appear together.

The name Bartholomew is actually a family name, meaning the "son of Tholmai." It was a common practice to place the word "bar", meaning "son of" after the first name, followed by the name of the father. (Bar-Tholmai – son of Tholmai, or Bartholomaios in the Greek).

Therefore, on this evidence, it is believed that Bartholomew was the second name of the apostle Nathanael.

Nathanael Bartholomew was a native of Cana in Galilee (John 21:2). This was the city where Jesus performed his first public miracle, changing water into wine at a marriage ceremony. Cana was near Nazareth where Jesus lived – this is the information Philip gave Nathanael when he told him that he had found the one Moses and the prophets wrote about: "Jesus of Nazareth" (John 1:45).

Nathanael was introduced to Jesus

(John 1:45-46)

Philip introduced Nathanael to Jesus. Philip told Nathanael, "*We have found the one Moses wrote about in the Law, and about whom the prophets also wrote - Jesus of Nazareth, the son of Joseph*" (John 1:45). Philip draws Nathanael's attention by describing Jesus, the One he had met, as the One the prophets wrote about.

This reminds us of what Jesus said to the disciples after His resurrection. "*How foolish you are, and how slow of heart to believe all that the prophets have spoken! Did not the Christ have to suffer these things and then enter his glory? Beginning with Moses and all the prophets, he explained to them what was said in all the Scriptures concerning himself*" (Luke 24:25-27). This shows the importance of studying the Old Testament, which is often neglected, for it clearly teaches about Christ.

It is generally accepted that Nathanael was a friend of Philip and knew enough about him to know he had knowledge of the scriptures and would be interested to hear the news - the One prophesied by Moses and the prophets had come.

Nathanael has doubts about Nazareth

Even though Nathanael would have studied the Old Testament Scriptures, he seemed reluctant to believe the exciting news that Philip brought to him. He asked, "*Can any good thing come out of Nazareth?*" (v.46). The one thing Nathanael heard that seemed to concern him a great deal was not that Jesus was referred to as "the son of Joseph" but that He was "Jesus of Nazareth."

It has been suggested that Nathanael may have resented the idea that the Messiah was from a neighbouring village rather than his own. His studies of the Old Testament had given him no suggestion that the Messiah would come from Nazareth. Nazareth is never mentioned in the Old Testament and according to the prophet Micah, the Messiah would come from Bethlehem, which was fulfilled (Micah 5:2). Nazareth, the place where Joseph had his carpenter's shop and where Jesus grew up, was a very small and relatively isolated village in Galilee. It had the reputation of being a rather immoral and unrefined village. Hence, it was thought that Jerusalem, the capital of Judea, rather than Nazareth, would have been a more suitable place from which the Messiah would come.

We also know that in Jesus' day there was prejudice towards certain places and groups of people. There was an assumption that important people came from certain areas, while those from other areas were somehow inferior. For Nathanael, coming from Nazareth was not in Jesus' favour.

Perhaps another reason for Nathanael's reluctance to accept the news from Philip was Nazareth's close proximity to Cana, his home village. Andrew and Peter came from Bethsaida and James and John were from Capernaum, all nearby. Given how close these small villages were to each other, it may have been difficult for Nathanael to accept that the Messiah should come from a very humble neighbouring village.

Nathanael reveals his prejudice

It would appear that Nathanael was displaying his unfavourable opinion of Nazareth. Do we judge people from the town in which they grew up, or the family they were born into? Making generalizations about people is very wrong. Prejudice, discrimination and bigotry are problems that have afflicted the human race for many generations. To think that one person is better than another because of where they were born has led to much fighting and many wars.

Comparing ourselves with others is condemned in scripture. Jesus said, "*Stop judging by mere appearances, and make a right judgement*" (John 7:24). "*You hypocrite, first take the plank out of your own eye, and then you will see clearly to remove the speck from your brother's eye*" (Matthew 7:5). If we want to compare ourselves with anyone, we need to compare ourselves to Jesus Christ. If we did that, circumstances would be radically different and the pride factor would not be part of our lives.

Nathanael had reservations as to whether he should believe that Jesus was the Messiah, but Philip was very wise in his counsel. He said, "*Come and see.*" Do we know someone with reservations as to whether they should believe what they have heard about Jesus? If so, then we also should take to heart the good advice of Philip and say to them 'come and see' for yourself and you will be amazed what you discover.

If we are seeking to win others for Jesus Christ then we too should never be afraid to speak to people who have doubts and fears about what to believe, as Philip spoke to Nathanael. Let us with confidence invite them to "*Taste and see that the Lord is good*" (Psalm 34:8).

Whatever the reasoning behind Nathanael's question, we find that Philip did not attempt to give an answer. He simply told him, "Come and see." He had confidence that the One whom he was talking about would be able to prove He was the Messiah and explain everything.

Nathanael's amazing discovery

(John 1:47-51)

As Jesus saw Nathanael coming with Philip, He said to those around Him, which Nathanael would have overheard, "*Here is a true Israelite, in whom there is nothing false*" (John 1:47). This statement surprised Nathanael for they had never met or spoken to each other, so how would Jesus have known anything about him.

Then Nathanael got another shock when Jesus told him, "*I saw you while you were still under the fig-tree before Philip called you*" (v.48). All Nathanael's prejudice and doubts were instantly removed and he declared, "*Rabbi, you are the Son of God; you are the King of Israel*" (v.49). Nathanael had doubts that the Messiah could come from such a place as Nazareth but as soon as he met Jesus, suspicion, doubts, prejudice and fears disappeared.

Jesus congratulates Nathanael

Right from the start, Nathanael recognised that there was something special about Jesus, just as Jesus had seen something special about Nathanael. Jesus wasn't physically present when Philip went to Nathanael so there was only one explanation - that Jesus was the Messiah, He was none other than the Son of God.

This was sure evidence that a Divine work had taken place in Nathanael's soul. This was only the second occasion when someone confessed Jesus as the Son of God – the first to do it was John the Baptist who declared, "*I have seen and I testify that this is the Son of God*" (John 1:34).

Jesus did not address Nathanael's doubts of His identity in the same way He addressed Thomas' doubt after His resurrection. On that occasion, Jesus said to Thomas, "*Put your finger here; see my hands. Reach out your hand and put it into my side. Stop doubting and believe*" (John 20:27). Instead, Jesus focuses on Nathanael's character, congratulating him for who he was - "a true Israelite."

Jesus was not talking about Nathanael's physical descent from Abraham. As an Israelite (Jew), Nathanael was distinguished from the people of other nations; and as a "*true Israelite without deceit*" he was distinguished from many of his own people who would not reach that standard.

Jesus said there was no pretence or deceit about Nathanael, no hypocrisy or sham. He was sincere and upright – an honest and pure-hearted believer. His devotion and love for God, and his desire to see the Messiah, were truly genuine. Jesus described Nathanael as an Israelite, "*in whom there is nothing false.*" These words echo King David's words in Psalm 32:1-2, "*Blessed is he whose transgressions are forgiven, whose sins are covered. Blessed is the man whose sin the Lord does not count against him and in whose spirit is no deceit.*"

Nathanael, a true Israelite

Paul taught there were two kinds of seed in Israel, the children of the flesh and the children of the promise (Romans 9:6-8). There is a difference between the natural seed of Abraham and the spiritual children of Abraham.

Abraham had two sons, Ishmael (by Hagar) and Isaac (by Sarah). Ishmael, the first-born should have been chosen, but God elected Isaac. Isaac had two sons Esau and Jacob, and Esau the first-born of the twins should have been chosen, but God elected Jacob. All were the natural descendants of Abraham but God did not base His election on human ancestry.

Paul also deals with this in Romans 2:28-29: *"A man is not a Jew if he is only one outwardly, ... No, a man is a Jew if he is one inwardly; ..."* Paul distinguishes between a Jew and a Jew. A person who is a Jew outwardly only, is a Jew by virtue of physical descent, nothing more; whereas the person who is a Jew not only outwardly but also inwardly is a genuine follower of Christ, whose heart is right with God.

Therefore, Jesus was saying that Nathanael was not a Jew (descendant of Israel) in name or flesh only, but spiritually alive to God, a genuine believer. Nathanael was a true and genuine Israelite, a sincere worshipper of God. He possessed the same spiritual faith as his forefathers who walked in the faith of Abraham and looked forward to the Messiah's coming.

Jesus was linking Nathanael's status as a true Israelite to the fact that he was without deceit, whereas many of the Israelites of Jesus' day were hypocrites, making the appearance only of living an upright life.

Jesus addressed the religious leaders of His day by saying, *"Woe to you, teachers of the law and Pharisees, you hypocrites ...."* (Matthew 23:13-33). Nathanael however, was real and Jesus knew this in spite of his reservations to Philip about the Messiah coming from Nazareth.

Is this not a rebuke to many in our generation who claim to be Christians, but are so in appearance and name only? Let us have no hypocrisy, no pretence and no sham in our lives. Let us prove by our lives and our lips that we are genuine believers in Jesus Christ, for He knows all about us. It would be marvellous to have Jesus' words of approval for our lives and for Him to say of us that we are true and genuine believers.

After Nathanael heard Jesus make the statement, *"Here is a true Israelite, in whom there is nothing false"* he asked, *"How do you know me?"* Nathanael must have been shocked with the answer he received, *"I saw you while you were still under the fig-tree before Philip called you"* (John 1:48).

Something special about Nathanael

We are not told what Nathanael was doing under the fig-tree. However, in Palestine the houses were small and to have privacy it was common to sit outside under the shade of the trees.

In biblical times, *"under the fig tree"* was a well known image for a place where somebody would go to think or study quietly. It was a good place for a person who liked to ponder things, because many houses in the first-century Palestine were primitive and had only one room, with little space for anything besides a place to sleep and a place to cook meals.

The fig-tree was a common tree to be planted outside the home giving fruit and shade. *"Every man will sit under his own vine and under his own fig-tree"* (Micah 4:4). *"In that day each of you will invite his neighbour to sit under his vine and fig-tree"* (Zechariah 3:10). *"During Solomon's lifetime, Judah and Israel, from Dan to Beersheba, lived in safety, each man under his own vine and fig-tree"* (1 Kings 4:25).

The common opinion is that Nathanael was "under the fig-tree" meditating on the Torah (the Jewish Scriptures) in privacy, while the leaves were providing shade from the sun. It is worth noting that it was not under 'a' fig-tree but under 'the' fig-tree. This leads us to believe that there was in Jesus' answer something that was highly significant to Nathanael - this was a particular tree. Was this the place where he would meditate and pray daily?

Do we have a special place set apart in our home (or outside the home) corresponding to Nathanael's fig-tree? A place where we can read and meditate on God's Word; a place where we can pray and refresh our soul; a place to wait before the Lord to renew our strength. Have you a "fig-tree"? Are you often found under it? Have you a quiet place which is blessed by the presence of God? Is that not what Jesus said, "*When you pray go into your room, close the door and pray to your Father, who is unseen. Then your Father who sees what is done in secret, will reward you*" (Matthew 6:6).

At this time, there were many devout people looking for the coming of the Messiah. Therefore, it is possible that when Philip called him, Nathanael was under the fig-tree praying for the speedy coming of the Messiah.

This incident shows us how Christ knows all about us; nothing can be hid from His all-seeing eye. Christ saw Nathanael and knew what he was doing even before Nathanael knew Jesus; and Christ has knowledge of us before we have knowledge of Him.

Every act, every deed, every place we go is known by the omniscient God. Like Adam and Eve when they ate the forbidden fruit, or Cain who killed his brother, or David who committed adultery, we cannot hide what we have done or are doing from the One who knows all things.

Nathanael recognised Jesus as the Son of God

Nathanael's immediate reply was *"You are the Son of God; you are the King of Israel."* These words are the expression of a heart convinced that Jesus was the Messiah. Had not Philip said to Nathanael, *"We have found the one Moses wrote about in the Law and about whom the prophets also wrote – Jesus of Nazareth, the son of Joseph"?* Nathanael expressed doubt and scepticism that anything good could come from Nazareth, but that all disappeared. He was now convinced because Jesus revealed He knew about Nathanael sitting under the fig-tree.

A similar situation took place when Jesus said to the woman of Samaria at the well, *"Go call your husband and come back."* She replied, *"I have no husband."* He answered, *"You are right when you say you have no husband. The fact is, you have had five husbands, and the man you now have is not your husband"* (John 4:17-18).

She ran into the village and declared, *"Come see a man who told me everything I ever did. Could this be the Christ?"* (John 4:29). The turning point in both cases was the conviction that Jesus knew what they were doing in secret, which is something we too should be aware of.

Nathanael's reply clearly shows that he, as well as Philip, was familiar with the Old Testament prophecies when he declared, *"You are the Son of God; you are the King of Israel."* The Psalmist spoke of the Messiah as being the Son of God (Psalm 2). Also many Old Testament prophets spoke of Him as "King of Israel."

When Micah was prophesying about His birth he said, *"But you, Bethlehem Ephrathah, though you are small among the clans of Judah, out of you will come for me one who will be ruler over Israel"* (Micah 5:2). When Zechariah was prophesying about

His death, he said, "*Rejoice greatly; O daughter of Zion! Shout, daughter of Jerusalem! See, your king comes to you, righteous and having salvation, gentle and riding on a donkey, on a colt, the foal of a donkey*" (Zechariah 9:9). Zephaniah said, "*The Lord has taken away your punishment, he has turned back your enemy. The Lord, the King of Israel, is with you; never again will you fear any harm*" (Zephaniah 3:15).

Nathanael, who studied the Scriptures, was waiting for the Messiah and knew that the One standing before him was none other than "*the Son of God and the King of Israel.*"

When the angel Gabriel came to Mary he told her, "*You will be with child and give birth to a son, and you are to give him the name Jesus. He will be great and will be called the Son of the Most High. The Lord God will give him the throne of his father David, and he will reign over the house of Jacob for ever; his kingdom will never end*" (Luke 1:31-33).

When Jesus was born the Magi from the East asked, "*Where is the one who has been born king of the Jews? We saw his star in the East and have come to worship him*" (Matthew 2:2). When Jesus was crucified the inscription over His head on the cross was, "*This is Jesus, the King of the Jews*" (Matthew 27:37).

When Jesus was dying on the cross the centurion, who was guarding Him, saw the earthquake and all that was happening and exclaimed, "*Surely he was the Son of God*" (Matthew 27:54).

One day Jesus will rule on David's throne over the gathered and restored tribes of Israel and will be acknowledged as the 'Son of God and the King of Israel.'

Nathanael shall see greater things
(John 1:50-51)

Jesus told Nathanael, *"You believe because I told you I saw you under the fig-tree. You shall see greater things than that"* (John 1:50). Jesus accepted Nathanael's statement that He was the Son of God and the King of Israel. As a reward for his faith, Jesus promised Nathanael that he would see even greater things than he had just experienced.

Jesus was just at the beginning of His earthly ministry and in the next three years Nathanael would see many miracles, hear much teaching and witness numerous evidences of His divine power and wisdom.

He would be at a wedding and see Jesus change water into wine; on a boat during a storm on the Sea of Galilee and see Jesus speak to the wind and the waves which would become still. He was going to be on a hillside where a huge crowd would be gathered and see Jesus break five loaves of bread and two fish, and multiply them until everyone was fed. Nathanael would be with Jesus at a place called Bethany where a man named Lazarus lay dead, and hear Jesus shout out, "Lazarus! Come out!" Nathanael would see Lazarus come out of that grave.

Nathanael was going to see Jesus, the Son of God, beaten and nailed to a cross and die. He was going to have first-hand knowledge of how Jesus was taken off that cross and put into a tomb. He would experience the frustration, the questions and the doubts of the apostles during those days. He was going to see the resurrected Jesus and the nail marks in His hands and hear Jesus' words, *"Peace be with you, do not be afraid."* He would witness these events with his own eyes and hear the words of Jesus with his own ears. We can now understand why Jesus said to him, *"You shall see greater things?"*

Nathanael will see heaven open

In v.50, the word "you" in *"you shall see greater things"* is singular and is addressed to Nathanael only. We have just discussed some of those greater things that Nathanael would personally see.

Nathanael received a personal promise for himself, but the truth Christ was about to express was for all the disciples who were present. The *"you shall see heaven open"* in v.51 is plural and was addressed to Nathanael and all those nearby.

Jesus said to Nathanael and those present, *"Truly, truly, you* (plural) *shall see heaven open ...."* The word 'truly' is twice repeated at the beginning of this sentence. It is found twenty-five times in the Gospel of John and always at the beginning of a sentence and always used by Jesus. It was used to emphasize some great and solemn truth, expressed as 'truly, truly' or 'most solemnly.'

Jesus said, *"Truly, truly, I tell you, you shall see heaven open, and the angels of God ascending and descending on the Son of Man."* The text says the angels ascended first. It does not say, "descending and ascending," as we might naturally suppose, but they ascended first because when Jesus was on earth they were already with Him. When Jesus Christ was on earth, He was never without His bodyguard of angels and these were His messengers to the courts above.

It is generally believed that Jesus' statement "the angels of God ascending and descending" is making reference to Jacob's dream in Genesis 28. Could it be that Nathanael was reading this passage when Jesus saw him under the fig-tree and He was now referring to it?

In the Old Testament, we have an account of Jacob as a

cunning, devious person who tricked his father into disinheriting his older brother in favour of himself. When his brother Esau found out, Jacob was afraid of what would happen to him and fled to his uncle Laban. On the way Jacob stopped for the night and lay down to sleep with a stone for a pillow. Then he had a dream in which he saw "*a ladder resting on the earth, with its top reaching to heaven; and the angels of God were ascending and descending on it*" (Genesis 28:12). It was then that the Lord identified Himself and promised that all peoples on earth will be blessed through Jacob and his offspring.

Jesus was a descendant of Jacob and was now referring to Himself as the ladder from earth to heaven through His redemptive work on the cross. Jesus said, "*I am the way and the truth and the life. No-one comes to the Father except through me*" (John 14:6). Nathanael and the others would come to see that Jesus was the 'Way' for sinful humanity to be reconciled to a holy God. To see Jesus as the 'Way' to heaven would be a thing far greater than even Jacob experienced.

Many people today are seeking to reach heaven by their own efforts, their good deeds and living, but that will prove unsuccessful. The only way to heaven that God has provided and will accept, is the person of His Son, Jesus Christ, who was without sin, took our sins on Himself and died on the cross. Do we believe that Jesus is the 'Way' for us to get to heaven?

Jesus reveals to Nathanael He is the Son of Man

Nathanael declared, "*Rabbi, you are the Son of God.*" Jesus Christ was the Son of God, fully God, one with His Father. However, that is not the whole story. Jesus was also a man, fully human, like us. He was born as a man, under the Law, through Mary. (See

Matthew 1:18, 20, 24-25; Galatians 4:4). Although His conception was miraculous, the scriptures make it clear that it did not prevent Him from being fully human. When Jesus was conceived, the Holy Spirit "came upon" His mother, resulting in His conception. The miracle was that God directly provided the seed for conception, making Jesus both the Son of God and also, as He was the son of Mary, fully human.

Because of His divine nature, God grants authority to Jesus to forgive sin and, because of His earthly purpose to be a ransom for many, He must suffer, be rejected, betrayed and killed, finally to rise again.

Jesus emphasized His humanity for different reasons on various occasions. Occasionally, He appears to have used the title "Son of Man" mainly to emphasize that He was human like us. On other occasions, Jesus used the title to emphasize his humanity as God's spokesman. Jesus came as a man to call sinners to repentance. *"For the Son of Man came to seek and to save what was lost"* (Luke 19:10).

Jesus also used the title "Son of Man" when speaking about His suffering, death and resurrection. He said that just as Jonah was three days and three nights in the belly of the fish as a sign to the Ninevites, *"so the Son of Man will be three days and three nights in the heart of the earth"* as a sign to His generation (Matthew 12:40). Jesus also told Peter, James and John not to tell anyone about His transfiguration *"until the Son of Man has been raised from the dead"* (Matthew 17:9).

Jesus was both God and man. Because Jesus was fully human, and lived His life on earth subject to the same pressures and temptations we face, He can sympathize with us in our trials, strengthen us, and make it possible for us to live as He did. We, therefore, have no excuse for our sins.

It is only because Jesus was a man like us that He could take our place, and His resurrection gives us hope for our resurrection. Jesus is able to bring us salvation, redemption, reconciliation with His Father and adoption as His children, only because He was a man who lived without sin and died for us. He now appears before His Father for us, as our advocate, because He is like us. If Jesus was not a man, we who believe in Him have nothing, and our faith is useless.

Traditional Views on Nathanael's final years

After His resurrection, Jesus appeared to some of His disciples, including Nathanael, by the Sea of Tiberias. Several of the disciples had returned to their old trade of fishing. In the morning Jesus appeared on the shore and asked them if they had caught any fish, to which they replied that they had not. Jesus told them to cast their net on the other side of the boat and when they did they caught a large number of fish (John 21:1-6).

The next reference to Nathanael is that he was among those present in the Upper Room when Jesus joined them behind closed doors (Acts 1:13).

According to tradition, after Christ's Death, Resurrection and Ascension, Nathanael Bartholomew evangelized in the East, in Mesopotamia, Persia, around the Black Sea, and perhaps reaching as far as India.

A popular tradition among the people of Armenia is that the apostle Jude (Thaddaeus) was the first to evangelize their region throughout the years of AD 43 to 66 and that the apostle Nathanael joined him in AD 60 bringing with him a copy of Matthew's Gospel written in Hebrew.

Eusebius, the historian (c AD 263 – 339) and Jerome, best known for his translation of the Bible into Latin (the Vulgate) (c AD 347 – 420), tell us that Nathanael had preached in India. They also tell us of a scholar by the name of Pantanaeus who, at the request of a native community there, was sent to India by Demetrius, bishop of Alexandria around AD 180. When Pantanaeus arrived, he was amazed to find a copy of the Gospel of Matthew, written in Hebrew, which had reportedly been brought there by the apostle Nathanael.

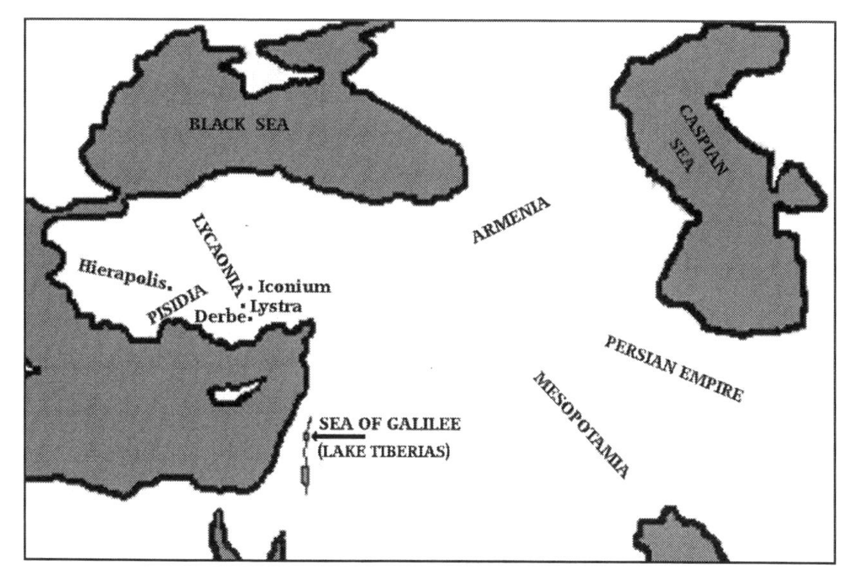

Map of places Nathanael visited

Both Jerome and Chrysostom - (John Chrysostom 347–407, Archbishop of Constantinople, an important Early Church Father) wrote that the apostle preached for a time in Lycaonia, before moving on to Armenia. Lycaonia was a region in central Asia Minor (now a part of Turkey).

We learn from the book of Acts that Paul and Barnabas preached there between AD 46 and 48 and that the most important cities were Derbe, Lystra and Iconium. At Iconium,

Paul and Barnabas found opposition from both Jews and Gentiles. Undeterred, Paul went to Derbe, where he and Barnabas were received more warmly.

After a brief stay, Paul retraced his steps through Lystra, Iconium, Antioch in Pisidia, and Perga, strengthening the believers along the way before returning by sea from the port of Attalia to Antioch in Syria. It is possible that Nathanael visited these cities at a later date and established additional congregations and ordained more elders.

Nathanael faithful to the end

It is also believed that Nathanael went to Hierapolis in Phrygia with the apostle Philip. This could only have taken place in AD 58 or 59 at the beginning of Philip's ministry there. It would have meant that he travelled west from Armenia into Asia Minor. He could not have stayed there very long, since it is quite likely that he reached India by AD 60.

Another tradition has it that while in India, Nathanael came upon the daughter of king Polymius. It was a heartbreaking situation where she was mentally-ill, and because she was so violent and would bite anyone near her, she was kept in a cage. Polymius, having heard of Nathanael's reputation as a holy man, begged him to help his daughter. When Nathanael insisted that the girl be released, everyone who knew her was afraid of what she would do. When she was released, Nathanael healed her and, as a result, Polymius allowed him to preach the Gospel freely in his territory.

Nathaniel Bartholomew is reported to have done many other wonderful things there and this exposed the worthlessness of the king's idols. Polymius and many others were baptised but the priests were very hostile to Nathanael because of what he was doing. They went to king Astyages of Babylon who was the brother of king Polymius to complain. King Astyages had Nathanael arrested, severely beaten with clubs and crucified head downwards. Nathanael died a martyr for his Lord in the year AD 68.

Nathanael was a man who expressed his doubts as to who Jesus was but this did not blind him to accepting the Saviour. When he accepted Philip's invitation to "Come and see," he was open to investigate and accept the evidence that was presented to him.

From a man who asked, "*can anything good come from Nazareth?*" we have a man who was deeply impressed by the One he met. Nathanael had an open mind and was prepared to overcome his prejudice and be proved wrong. As a result, he became a faithful and dedicated disciple of Jesus Christ.

Though Nathanael was an honest man, he was made aware of his need of a Saviour. He discovered that Jesus was the 'ladder' to heaven, and that He is the only way. As we study the life of Nathanael, we see how God can take a person who has reservations about spiritual things and change that life to be a person of strong faith and a mighty disciple for Christ.

Thomas
THE ONE WHO EXPRESSED HIS DOUBTS

All four Gospels have Thomas in the list of the apostles of Jesus. Matthew and Mark mention him only once (Matthew 10:3; Mark 3:18). Luke lists him once in his Gospel and in Acts (Luke 6:15; Acts 1:13). John gives eight references to Thomas as a disciple of Jesus.

In John 11:16, Thomas is also called "Didymus" which means "the twin." Thomas may have had a twin brother or sister, but the scriptures do not say who this was. Some suggest that Thomas' real name was Judah, and since two other disciples are called by that name, he was called "the twin" to identify him from the others.

We know nothing of when and how Thomas was called to become a disciple. He was a Jew and like the other faithful apostles, probably a Galilean (Acts 1:11). Since he was with the other disciples fishing, after Christ was crucified, he probably was a fisherman (John 21:2).

Thomas is most often remembered for his doubting, due to the fact that he was missing from the Upper Room when Jesus appeared to the disciples after His Resurrection. When the disciples told Thomas about Jesus appearing to them he refused to believe it and made this statement, *"Unless I see the nail marks in his hands and put my finger where the nails were, and put my hand into his side, I will not believe it"* (John 20:25).

Although Thomas expressed his doubt very forcibly at this time, once he saw the risen Lord, his loyalty and dedication was exceptional in the years to follow. He proved to be a man of great faith and courageous zeal for his beloved Lord.

A courageous Thomas

(John 11:1-16)

Apart from Thomas being mentioned in the list of twelve apostles in all four Gospels, John is the only one to give us some details of his ministry. The first mention is given just after the death of Lazarus. A message had been sent to tell Jesus that His friend Lazarus, the brother of Martha and Mary, was sick, but Jesus delayed going to see him for two days. Then Jesus told His disciples that He was going to see Lazarus who had "fallen asleep," but the disciples replied, *"Lord if he sleeps, he will get better"* (John 11:12). Jesus had to tell them plainly, *"Lazarus is dead,"* adding, *"I am glad I was not there, so that you may believe."*

The disciples were not happy that Jesus should return to Bethany, near Jerusalem. They had recently come from that area where the Jews had tried to stone Jesus accusing Him of blasphemy and therefore, He was facing great danger in returning. But Jesus insisted in going back, and the disciples knew that they could not change His mind, so at this point Thomas spoke to the other disciples, *"let us also go, that we may die with him."*

Does this show Thomas as being pessimistic, expecting the worst? Some commentators believe that he was saying, "let us go and die with Lazarus." However, it is widely believed that Thomas was saying to the other disciples that they should go with Jesus back to the area where the Jews had threatened to kill Him and be prepared to face death.

Could this be a statement of unbelief, despair and gloom, seeing nothing but danger and failure? Remember Thomas showed the same concerns when Jesus said He was going to prepare a place for them. Thomas said to Jesus, *"Lord, we don't know where you are going, so how can we know the way?"* (John 14:5).

After Jesus' death and resurrection, Thomas was not present when Jesus appeared to His disciples. Again, Thomas displayed his uncertainty and concern when he said, *"Unless I see the nail marks in his hands and put my finger where the nails were, and put my hand into his side, I will not believe it"* (John 20:25). On each occasion, Thomas was looking at the dark side of things expressing doubt, fear and despair as he faced the unknown.

Here we see Thomas' loyalty to Jesus, and though he was pessimistic about the future and the almost certainty of facing death, he was prepared to go and face it. He did not want to live without Jesus, and if Jesus was going to die, he was prepared to die with Him.

It is wonderful to know that our salvation does not depend on our feelings. We are often like Thomas and have periods of fear, doubt and despair, but when we have committed our lives to Christ we have that sure and certain hope of eternal life with Christ in heaven.

It is comforting to know that, in spite of his doubts, in later years Thomas became a great evangelist for his Saviour.

A Puzzled Thomas
(John 14:1-7)

The second incident recorded by John concerning Thomas takes place in the Upper Room. It was there that Jesus met with His disciples for the Passover meal before His crucifixion. Though Jesus had often told the disciples of His approaching death, it would appear they had no idea that Jesus was soon to be crucified and when He told them He was about to leave them, it came as a great shock.

John chapter 14 records the occasion when Jesus was with His disciples for the last time, He told them what heaven was like and what He was going to do when He left them. He was going to prepare a place for them for the day when they would join Him. He instructed them not to be troubled and to trust in God.

It is reasonable to believe that most, if not all, of the disciples were puzzled and did not know what Jesus was trying to tell them, in spite of the fact that they had been with Him for three years. No one seemed to have the courage to show their ignorance and ask Jesus what He meant; even the usually bold Peter did not speak up. We are reminded in scripture, "*You do not have, because you do not ask God*" (James 4:2).

It was Thomas who expressed the concerns of them all by asking the question, "*Lord, we don't know where you are going, so how can we know the way*" (John 14:5)? Jesus had just told His close friends who had been with Him for the past three years, "*My children, I will be with you only a little longer. You will look for me, and just as I told the Jews, so I tell you now: Where I am going, you cannot come*" (John 13:33).

Jesus was telling them He was leaving them very soon,

and they could not go with Him. Understandably that was hard to accept, and naturally they wanted to know where He was going and how they could go to be with Him.

Thomas is told Jesus is 'the Way' to heaven

As we have already seen, Thomas was not a man who would take things at face value and be satisfied without knowing the details. However, we are eternally grateful to Thomas for asking the question, for we now have a very clear answer from Jesus how we too can get to heaven. He said, *"I am the way and the truth and the life. No-one comes to the Father except through me"* (John 14:6).

The word that is translated "way" comes from the Greek word '*hodos*', meaning 'way,' 'road' or 'highway'. The same word is used in Matthew 2:12 where we are told how the Magi, after visiting the baby Jesus, had been warned in a dream not to go back to Herod, "*they returned to their country by another route*" (way).

It can be troubling and frustrating to want to reach somewhere we have heard about, but do not know the way to go. But here Jesus was telling the disciples that He was the true "road," "highway" or "route" that leads to His "Father's house." Jesus was saying, I am the way, and there is no other. Christ is the "way" to heaven and to have peace with God.

Many people are displeased and upset when they are told that Jesus is the ONLY way to heaven. They say faith is an individual matter and every view is equally valid. It is intolerant and arrogant to insist that Jesus is the only way rather than one of many ways.

There are those who believe we live in a multi-faith society, and there are many faiths and religions, all of which have equal value before God. However, the difference between Christianity and other religions is the fact that Christianity proclaims the deity, death and resurrection of Jesus Christ, whereas other faiths deny one or all of these scripture truths.

Another major difference is that Christianity is the only religion that proclaims salvation through grace alone and not of works. Other religions emphasize the need for people to do something towards their salvation and, as a result, they struggle to earn the favour of God.

Jesus made it plain that no one gets to heaven or to the Father except through Him. To reach God in heaven we must go through Christ as He is the Mediator between God and man. Sin is so sinful in God's sight that no person can do anything, or pay anything, to satisfy divine justice. Therefore, no one can be saved through his or her own efforts or own religion. Whoever will enter into heaven must be saved, and without the shed blood of Jesus Christ there is no cleansing and forgiveness.

Thomas is told, Jesus is 'the Truth' about God

Jesus is the "way" to God; He is also the "truth." He has come to tell the truth about the Father, He said *"I am the Truth."* When Jesus stood before Pilate, He said, *"I came into the world, to testify to the truth."* Pilate asked him, 'What is truth?' That is the question often asked today. Jesus said, 'I am the truth.' People may misunderstand the truth of the Christian gospel; they may resent it, they may ridicule it, and others may distort it, but the truth is absolute. Jesus is the whole substance of truth.

Jesus is "the Life" for everyone who believes in Him. Christ is the author and giver of life, natural, spiritual, and eternal; He is the way of life. On another occasion, He said, *"I am the bread of life"* (John 6:35). Christ is the one who gives life, this is what

He taught in John 3:16 *"For God so loved the world, that he gave his only begotten Son, that whosoever believeth in him should not perish, but have eternal life."* This is an amazing statement – believe in Christ and you have everlasting life. Jesus said, *"I have come that they may have life, and have it to the full"* (John 10:10).

We are greatly indebted to Thomas for asking the question, *"Lord, we don't know where you are going, so how can we know the way,"* because we have been given the clear declaration from Christ about the way to heaven.

Thomas missed an opportunity to meet Jesus

(John 20:19-24)

The third incident recorded by John concerning Thomas takes place near the end of the first Easter day. Several people had seen Jesus that morning, but later the disciples met in fear and uncertainty. As they talked and shared with each other the recent events, in spite of the doors being locked, Jesus suddenly appeared among them. On that occasion, all the disciples, except Thomas, were present. This incident reveals what a Christian may unexpectedly lose by not meeting with other believers. The writer to the Hebrews challenges us, *"Let us not give up meeting together, as some are in the habit of doing, but let us encourage one another"* (Hebrews 10:25).

There may have been a genuine reason why Thomas was absent. However, in the light of the life-changing events which had shattered the world of Jesus' closest friends, it seems unlikely that he should be involved in anything more important than meeting with his brethren.

Thomas may have wanted to be alone in his grief and not able to face being with the other disciples. Nevertheless, by missing this meeting with the other disciples on the first day of the week, Thomas missed a great blessing. Under the circumstances, he should have been with the other disciples. We are told that Jesus showed the disciples His hands and His side and they were *"overjoyed when they saw the Lord."*

We do not know when the disciples saw Thomas to tell him the good news that they had seen the risen Saviour. It could have been that very day, with the result he was left in doubt, suspense and unbelief for a week wondering if it was really true that Christ had risen from the dead. The other disciples, however, were rejoicing in that they had seen and heard the risen Saviour.

What Thomas missed by not seeing Jesus

i) Thomas missed the reunion with Jesus. Perhaps Thomas missed that meeting because he thought it not worthwhile, believing that Jesus was now dead and did not expect Him to have risen from the dead? But sad to say, after living and travelling with Him for three years, Thomas missed a wonderful opportunity for a re-union with his Master. Is this the reason why many people do not attend a place of worship on Sunday – they do not expect to meet Christ? If so, like Thomas, they miss a wonderful experience for Jesus said, "*Where two or three come together in my name, there am I with them*" (Matthew 18:20).

ii) Thomas missed hearing the words of Jesus. We are told that Jesus said to the disciples, "*Peace be with you.*" When Jesus spoke of 'peace' to His disciples He was speaking of having peace with God. We are separated from God because of sin. Scripture says, "*Your iniquities have separated you from your God*" (Isaiah 59:2). But because of Christ's death on the cross and His resurrection, sin can be removed and we can have peace with God. Paul writing to the Romans says, "*Therefore, since we have been justified through faith, we have peace with God through our Lord Jesus Christ*" (Romans 5:1).

Not only does Jesus offer us peace with God, He also offers us the peace of God. The Bible speaks of this peace when it says, "*And the peace of God, which transcends all understanding, will guard your hearts and your minds in Christ Jesus*" (Philippians 4:6-7). After the momentous events that the disciples had so recently experienced, the offer of knowing peace with God and also enjoying the peace of God was so appropriate.

Thomas missed out in all this and we can miss out in this experience when we neglect "assembling together with other believers."

Many people today are like the disciples. They are anxious and troubled about their present situation and also about the future. Therefore, to hear words of comfort from the Saviour would surely calm the troubled soul. Thomas missed those words of comfort and had to wait for another week before he would hear them from the Saviour.

No doubt Jesus also explained to the disciples many things concerning Himself as He did to the two disciples on the road to Emmaus. On that occasion they said, "*Were not our hearts burning within us while he talked with us on the road and opened the Scriptures to us?*" (Luke 24:32).

Thomas missed hearing the scriptures explained to him and that also is the situation for the believer who, without a genuine reason, is absent from their place of worship.

iii) Thomas missed the Christian fellowship. In Acts 2:42 we read that one of the four things the early church devoted itself to, was "fellowship". *"They devoted themselves to the apostles' teaching and to the fellowship, to the breaking of bread and to prayer."* Fellowship was a very important reason for meeting together.

We speak of having fellowship as people meet together with common interests, or for a meal, but church fellowship is something more meaningful and special. Christian fellowship occurs when two or more Christians are in one another's company. Christian fellowship is essential. Being in the company of other Christian people is very important to our growth and survival as Christians. Thomas missed the Christian fellowship and sad to say, so do many Christians today because of their failure to worship with other believers on the Sabbath Day.

iv) Thomas missed the joy of seeing Jesus. We are told the disciples *"were overjoyed when they saw the Lord."* The disciples were disillusioned and discouraged in the aftermath of Jesus' death and apparent defeat. They were a sad and downhearted group who met behind locked doors for fear of the Jews.

When Jesus stood among them all fear disappeared and they were filled with joy. Many people have often gone to their place of worship with a heavy and troubled soul and have returned uplifted and rejoicing because of the experience they had encountered during the service.

v) Thomas missed seeing the evidence he wanted. When the other disciples told Thomas that they had seen Jesus, Thomas said, *"Unless I see the nail marks in his hands and put my finger where the nails were, and put my hand into his side, I will not believe it"* (v.25). If Thomas had been present on that first Sunday with the other disciples he would have seen these things for we are told, *"he showed them his hands and side"* (v.20).

vi) Thomas missed the commission from Jesus. The disciples

were afraid and met behind locked doors, but Jesus told them to have no fear and offered them peace 'with' God and the peace 'of' God. When they experienced this peace they were able to go out and be witnesses for Christ. Jesus said, *"Peace be with you, as the Father sent me even so send I you."* Jesus then sent them out as His ambassadors.

Jesus was sent into the world by the Father so 'we' are now sent into the world by Jesus. In His prayer to the Father Jesus said, *"As you sent me into the world, I have sent them into the world"* (John 17:18).

Thomas was not present for this vitally important commission and many today are not aware that Christ has given them a similar commission, as they lack a full understanding of the teaching of scripture.

Many Christians are doing nothing to evangelize this world. God the Father sent Jesus into the world to save the world through Him. Have they not heard because we fail to tell? If we would go into the world as Christ went into the world, lives would be changed.

Thomas demanded evidence

(John 20:24-25)

Thomas was absent the first time Jesus appeared to the disciples after His resurrection. When the other disciples told him about it he refused to believe and so this incident more than any is the one that gives Thomas the nick-name 'doubting Thomas.'

Thomas was determined that he would not accept the resurrection of Jesus without proof. He was so convinced that Jesus was still dead that nothing would satisfy him except a personal and physical encounter. The very form of his statement shows how convinced he was. Notice he did not say 'If I see, I will believe' but rather his statement was *"Unless I see, I will not believe."* This was an emotional time for everyone and these words could well show a man who was so devastated that he had missed the event that others had experienced. If he had only been present with the other disciples the first time Jesus appeared, he would have seen all the evidence he wanted.

However, it is unfair to criticize Thomas too severely for expressing his unbelief. Is there not evidence that the other disciples also experienced unbelief? We are told what happened when the women returned from the tomb after finding the stone rolled away, *"When they came from the tomb, they told all these things to the Eleven and to all the others. But they did not believe the woman because their words seemed to them like nonsense"* (Luke 24:9-11).

In Luke's account of what happened when Jesus appeared to the disciples we are told, *"They were startled and frightened, thinking they saw a ghost. He said to them, 'Why are you troubled, and why do doubts rise in your minds? Look at my hands and my feet. It is I myself! Touch me and see; a ghost does not have flesh and bones, as you see I have'"* (Luke 24:37-38).

Therefore, all of the disciples thought Jesus rising from the dead was impossible, so it is unfair to single out Thomas as the only one with doubts about Jesus' resurrection.

However, Thomas had heard the testimony of the women and Mary Magdalene. He had also heard the report from John and Peter regarding the empty tomb and the grave clothes. He did not even accept the testimony of the other apostles, nor the two disciples who met Jesus on the road to Emmaus and others who were present (Luke 24:33-34).

This shows us the honesty of the scriptures, when it is recorded that even Jesus' close disciples did not at first believe that He had risen from the dead.

Christ had chosen the apostles to be His special witnesses of His life, death and resurrection, to the nations of the world, yet Thomas one of that group, was refusing to believe. If Thomas could not believe the testimony of his own colleagues and friends, how then were they supposed to convince others of the truth of the gospel?

Thomas met the resurrected Jesus

(John 20:26-29)

No one needed to tell Jesus what Thomas had said for on the next Sabbath day Jesus again appeared to the disciples and immediately said to Thomas, *"Put your finger here, see my hands. Reach out your hand and put it into my side. Stop doubting and believe"* (v.27). He was answering the very conditions that Thomas had demanded.

Whether Thomas did actually touch our Lord's wounds, as he was told to do, is an open question which we have no means of knowing. There is no evidence or proof that he did; his exclamation reads as if it was sudden and immediate and not the result of examination or investigation. We notice Jesus said to him, *"Because you have seen me, you have believed; blessed are those who have not seen and yet have believed"* (John 20:29).

When Thomas saw Jesus, he cried out, *"My Lord and my God"* (v.28). Thomas was now in no doubt, he had seen with his own eyes that Jesus had risen from the dead and immediately recognised the deity of Christ. The divinity of Christ is one of the foundational truths of Christianity. It is a fundamental truth of the Christian faith that is consistently taught in the Bible.

Jesus gave an important statement to Thomas, and to all who may have doubts and unbelief in His resurrection. There would be many in the years to come who would wrestle with the same question about the genuineness of the resurrection. What Jesus said to Thomas applies to every doubter in every generation. Thomas and others reported what they had seen and because of this we have the confidence to believe in our generation.

Historians today are seeking to reject Jesus as being historical. Not only do we have the New Testament as proof of the history of Jesus, but there are plenty of non-biblical sources proving that Jesus Christ existed.

He lived on this earth, He was crucified and He rose again. *"Blessed are those who have not seen and yet have believed"* (John 20:29).

Thomas' final days

The next reference we have about Thomas is when Jesus appeared again to his disciples by the Sea of Tiberias (John 21:1-14). Several of the disciples had decided to go fishing and after fishing all night they caught nothing. In the morning Jesus stood on the shore but the disciples did not realise that it was Jesus. He asked them if they had caught any fish and they replied that they had caught nothing. Jesus told them to throw the net on the other side of the boat. Despite being seasoned fishermen themselves, the disciples were willing to be guided by this unrecognised stranger.

As a result they were unable to haul the net in because of the large number of fish caught in it. After this miracle we are told, *"None of the disciples dared ask him, 'Who are you?' They knew it was the Lord"* (John 21:12).

The next reference regarding Thomas was when the disciples returned to Jerusalem after Christ's ascension into heaven. They were waiting there for the coming of the Holy Spirit (Acts 1:13). After Pentecost, we learn from the writer Eusebius that Thomas was involved in evangelising the nation of Osroane, which lay to the north of Palestine in what is now eastern Turkey, between the Roman and Iranian Empires.

According to Church Tradition, Thomas founded churches in Palestine, Mesopotamia, Parthia, Ethiopia and India. The exact route that he took is not clear, but it is believed that on the way to India he established churches in the Yemen. This church was destroyed around AD 600 by the advance of Islam.

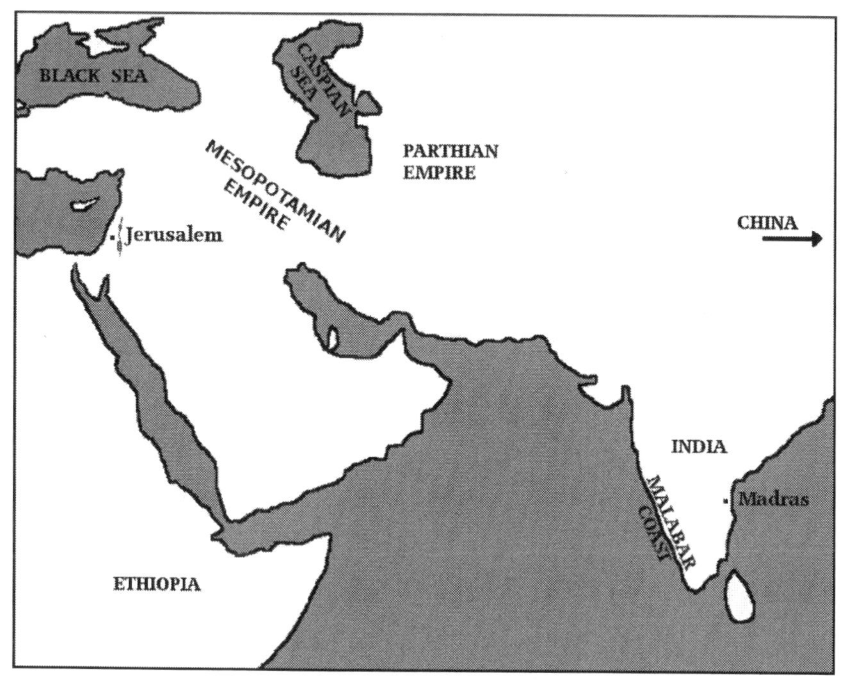

Map of places Thomas visited

Clement of Alexandria (c. AD 150 - c.215) made a passing reference to St. Thomas' Apostolate in Parthia. Eusebius of Caesarea (c. AD 263 – 339) quoted Origen (he was an early Christian Alexandrian scholar and theologian, and one of the most distinguished writers of the early Church) as saying, "When the Apostles and disciples were scattered over all the world, Thomas, so tradition had it, obtained his portion, Parthia ..." At its height in the first century BC, this empire occupied areas in what is now Iran, Iraq, Turkey, Armenia, Georgia, Azerbaijan, Turkmenistan, Afghanistan, Tajikistan, Pakistan, Syria, Lebanon, Jordan, Palestine and Israel.

Thomas is traditionally believed to have set out from Jerusalem in the company of Bartholomew and Jude Thaddaeus. While Bartholomew and Thaddaeus remained in the Middle East, Thomas arrived at the west coast of India in AD 49, stayed briefly and then went to China where he founded a church in Peking. We cannot prove Thomas was in China, neither can we disprove this convincing tradition.

On returning to India he was the means of spreading the Christian faith among the Jews who had been dispersed and living in Kerala on the south-west of India at that time. Thomas is said to have preached the gospel throughout the Malabar Coast, preaching to all classes of people and had many converts, including members of the four principal castes in India. From AD 59 onwards, he began to travel through south India founding Christian colonies in cities throughout the region.

History records that fourteen centuries later, when Portuguese explorers were making the first contacts between Europe and Asia, they were surprised to encounter on the coast of India a community of Christians. These believers traced their origins to the ministry of Thomas. Archaeological finds have indicated that Christianity in India goes back at least to the second century.

Extensive trade relations existed between Malabar, India and the Mediterranean countries even before the Christian era. The most direct route to India in the first century was via Alexandria and the Red Sea taking advantage of the Monsoon winds, which could carry ships directly to and from the Malabar coast.

In the light of the traditions which have a great deal of history to back them up, we can confidently reconstruct the journeys of Thomas. Many early Christian writings exist about Thomas' mission. St. Jerome (342- 420) wrote, "He (Christ) dwelt in all places: with Thomas in India and Paul in Illyricum."

Early in AD 62, Thomas started a long series of missionary tours, similar to those that the Apostle Paul had conducted in the Near East a few years earlier, and in AD 69 he settled permanently in Mylapore. According to most Indian traditions Thomas died of stab wounds in AD 72. The Brahman priests of Mylapore feared that Christianity would overtake Hinduism. Several of their number found Thomas praying in a cave near his home on a hill in Mylapore, a suburb of Madras, India, and attacked him inflicting fatal wounds with a spear. Thomas was buried near the site of his death.

It is accepted as fact that some of his remains were later, in the 13th century, moved to Edessa, Mesopotamia and then later taken by ship to Ortona, Italy.

Doubting Thomas became a faithful disciple.

It is clear that Thomas, who as a disciple was puzzled about Christ's resurrection and demanded evidence that it was true, became a vigorous missionary. The evidence from tradition and early church records has grown so great, concerning his mission to Babylon, Persia and India, that it must be accepted as convincing.

Thomas was a courageous evangelist and a great builder of churches. No one can estimate how many came to faith in Christ because of Thomas. There are churches in India today who trace their roots to the early work of Thomas.

The traditional history of the missionary journeys of Thomas shows him to be a most active and convincing defender of the Gospel of Christ. He fearlessly entered such godless lands as India, Babylon and Persia to preach boldly for his Lord.

It is amazing how someone who was called 'doubting Thomas' could be changed by an encounter with Christ and be mightily used by God for the extension of His kingdom. May we also seek Christ for our lives and be amazed by what God can do through us.

Thomas has much to teach us about how to process truths and come to authentic conclusions. He was humble enough to admit that when he did not know something, he was prepared to ask questions. Thomas was willing to change his mind, when new evidence was presented to him.

Our spiritual experiences through faith can be just as compelling as the experiences of Thomas, when he bowed before the incarnate Jesus and said with genuine convictions, *"My Lord and my God."*

Thomas has left us with the most vigorous and committed confession of faith to be found in the New Testament, *"My Lord and my God."* Therefore he should not be remembered as a 'doubter' but for his faith and zeal.

Matthew
the Tax Collector

Matthew is the author of the Gospel that bears his name. For that reason, we might expect to have more information about this man and his character. The fact of the matter is that we know very little about him. In his entire Gospel, he mentions his own name only twice - where he records his call (Matthew 9:9) and when he lists all twelve disciples (Matthew 10:3). The apostle Matthew, also called Levi, was the son of Alphaeus (Mark 2:14), and because the apostle James is also the son of a man named Alphaeus (Matthew 10:3), it has been thought that he and James were brothers. The two were never referred to as brothers, whereas Peter and Andrew; James (a different James) and John, were consistently referred to as being brothers. Nothing else is known about James except that he was among those who went to the upper room to pray after the Ascension of Jesus.

In his own Gospel, Matthew calls himself the tax collector (10:3), but the other Gospel writers omit his shameful profession (Mark 3:18; Luke 6:15). By mentioning his type of work, Matthew was confessing how unworthy and unlikely a candidate he was to be an apostle of the Lord Jesus Christ.

As empires go, Rome was most cruel in the way it dealt with its conquered subjects. Taxation was handled by "appointing" a local person to collect taxes for Rome. However, this appointment was really a position that went to the highest bidder. So, not only was this person collecting taxes from his own people for the occupying army, but he paid Rome for the privilege. Some of the taxes levied on the Jewish people might have been oppressive in themselves, but sometimes it was the tax collectors who made the situation unduly difficult by collecting more than was due and pocketing the difference. We know this because at one point, when John the Baptist called for repentance, he warned the tax collectors to stop this practice (Luke 3:12-13). Other details in scripture equate tax collectors with prostitutes, heathens and other sinners (Matthew 9:10; 11:19; 18:17; 21:31), so clearly they were not well regarded and tax collecting was among the most hateful of trades.

Moreover, they were disqualified as witnesses in courts of law, scoffed at as common criminals, and refused admittance to the synagogue, where their money was also refused for alms. They were banished to the status of social lepers.

As the taxation burden became ever more intolerable, so the tax collectors became more hateful and dreaded people. Being so unpopular, the collectors' job was no easy one; indeed at times they ran great personal risk, as angry people were quite likely to lynch them. With the power of the Roman Empire behind them, enforced by the presence of Roman soldiers, tax collectors could threaten the people into paying excessive fees. While the commoners suffered because of these taxes, the tax collectors often became wealthy.

Fiercely disliked by the general public, tax collectors were divided into two classes. One group, the *gabbai* or general tax collectors, collected taxes on wine, fruit and similar items. The second group, to which Matthew belonged, was the *mikhsa* or customs house officials. They were despised because they could stop people and search them, looking for illegal imports or smuggled goods.

With his office just outside Capernaum, Matthew had an ideal location. The heavily loaded caravans moving on the main highway from Damascus to Jerusalem had to stop at his customs house and pay taxes on both imports and exports. Peter, Andrew and their partners, James and John may also have had to pay taxes on the fish they caught. In other words, these four men probably paid enormous amounts of money to Matthew prior to the time they joined together as disciples of Jesus Christ. It is no wonder it took these men time to develop trust and unity in their relationships.

The good news, however, is that tax collectors can be converted. Zacchaeus illustrates this point when he responded to Christ's call on his life, and he was transformed. We are told that Zacchaeus was a *"chief tax collector and was wealthy"* (Luke 19:2). Though Matthew is not identified as a "chief collector," he too was wealthy. The amazing thing is that even though this man was an outcast from society, Jesus Christ called him to be one of His chosen disciples.

Jesus calls Matthew

(Matthew 9:9; Mark 2:13-14; Luke 5:27-28)

All three Gospels link the healing of a paralytic to the call of Matthew. Jesus had entered a home in Capernaum and so many people had gathered that the house was full and a number remained outside the door. Some men brought a paralysed man to be healed but, as they could not enter the house, they made a hole in the roof and lowered the man down to Jesus. There, Jesus had said to the paralytic, *"Take heart, son; your sins are forgiven"* (Matthew 9:2). The paralytic was healed and when the crowd saw this *"they were filled with awe; and they praised God"* (v.8).

After this, Jesus saw Matthew sitting at the tax collectors' booth and said to him, *"Follow me"* (Matthew 9:9; Mark 2:14; Luke 5:27). Without delay, he rose and followed Jesus. Matthew gives no further details about this unforgettable experience. Luke, however, tells us *"Levi got up, left everything and followed him"* (Luke 5:28).

Mark and Luke call this man 'Levi'. He calls himself 'Matthew'. In all the lists of the apostles he is called Matthew (Matthew 10:3; Mark 3:18; Luke 6:15, Acts 1:13). We do not know when his name was changed from Levi to Matthew. Did Jesus give him this new name when the tax collector became a disciple, as the Lord had also changed Simon's name to Cephas (Peter), when the latter joined this group? (Mark 3:16; John 1:42) It is, however, possible that from the beginning he had two names, as may also have been true with respect to Thomas (John 11:16) and with Bartholomew and Nathanael who are one and the same person. (See Chapter 6, Nathanael Bartholomew)

When Jesus asked Matthew to follow Him he, no doubt, was shocked and overwhelmed at the invitation. Matthew immediately had the desire to follow Jesus. Perhaps he was aware of who Jesus was, knowing what had happened to the fishermen, James and John, who had left their nets and followed Jesus. Also, he may have been aware of what had happened in the house near him where a paralytic was lowered down through a hole in the roof of the house. The excitement that followed would not have escaped Matthew's attention and so, when Jesus called him to follow Him, he was prepared to do so.

Matthew experienced the wonderful grace of Jesus. No matter what kind of work he was involved in, or the reputation he may have had, he received complete forgiveness and was called to become a disciple.

Matthew's call by Jesus demonstrated the availability of forgiveness for the worst of people. Not just respectable and nice people are called to follow Jesus. God's love knows no bounds; His grace reaches to all. Others looked on Matthew with hate, Jesus saw a man who needed the gift of love and forgiveness for sin. This same gift is free to all who have sinned and turn to Christ in repentance.

Matthew made a clean break with his former occupation and joined the One who called him. Of course we should note that, since Matthew was a minor official, not the chief tax collector, the business of collecting the tax at Capernaum did not cease when he left all to follow Jesus. He left his profitable business and trusted God would provide for his needs in the future. Therefore, Matthew's sacrifice was much greater than that made by the four earlier disciples - Simon and Andrew, James and John. They were fishermen and could quite easily return to fishing, but to become re-employed as a collector for customs' duties was a completely different matter. He would have closed his accounts, satisfied the Roman Government and cleared his desk for his successor. We can see here that, with Christ, nothing is impossible. He can take a tax collector and make him an apostle. We should never despair of anyone's salvation.

Matthew invites Jesus to a Banquet

(Matthew 9:10-13; Mark 2:15-17; Luke 5:29-32)

Immediately after accepting Jesus' call, Matthew held a great feast in his own house in honour of Jesus, and invited a large crowd of tax collectors and others. The facts of the feast, the long list of invited guests, and a house and property spacious enough to accommodate the crowd, all point to Matthew's wealth. Though we are not told how many people attended, Luke would not have used the word "great" if this were not a huge affair. Matthew and Mark tell us "many" attended the dinner.

Since Matthew was a tax collector, it is no surprise that tax collectors were in the majority at this meal. Because of the nature of his job, he would have had few friends. Now that his life was changed as a result of meeting Jesus, Matthew wanted his former colleagues to meet Him. He probably did not know anyone high up the social ladder or from the upper class of society well enough to invite them to his house.

Perhaps many of those who joined Matthew for the dinner were curious and wanted to meet this person who had been the cause of Matthew leaving his well-paid job. Perhaps they even thought he was offered a better financial deal by Jesus. What other reason could be given for this sudden change of circumstances. The fact that so many of his associates accepted his invitation indicates the influence he held in the world of taxation.

Andrew brought his brother Simon to Jesus and Philip witnessed to Nathanael (John 1:41, 45) after they followed Jesus, showing their concern for their closest friends.

Matthew was so thrilled at the change that had taken place in his life, since he answered the call of Jesus, that he wanted to introduce Jesus to everyone he knew. So he invited them to a large banquet in Jesus' honour. It is good to see that Matthew's first social occasion after his conversion was one that centred on Jesus. Do we build our social activities around our religious life with the intention of bringing praise to Christ, or is it possible that our social life is still very questionable?

Matthew wanted to witness to his former colleagues, so he invited them to dinner. If he invited moral and righteous people, they may have avoided him, for only tax collectors and sinners would set foot in his house. Matthew was saying to his fellow-workers that he was leaving his job as a tax collector. He was making a public declaration to his friends of his intention of following Jesus. Matthew knew this would be an opportunity for any of them who may have wished to have a better way of life to find it in Jesus. So he gave his guests an opportunity to meet Him. The genuine Christian will earnestly desire that others may experience the call of Christ.

The Scribes and Pharisees grumbled and complained about Jesus. "*Why does your teacher eat with tax collectors and 'sinners'*" (Matthew 9:11). However, when Jesus heard those complaining, He reminded them that it is the sick who need a doctor, not the healthy, and when people realise that they are sinners, there is a Saviour to meet their need and save them. Jesus came into the world for fallen sinners and to heal the broken hearted and offer strength to the weak. Jesus did not meet with Matthew's friends to have a meal and entertainment. He was there to meet their spiritual needs and bring them to God.

Some people may consider themselves to be too great a sinner to be saved, but we can never be too great a sinner for the Lord Jesus to save. Paul said, "*Christ Jesus came into the world to save sinners; of whom I am the worst*" (1 Timothy 1:15). Therefore, we have the assurance that, as Christ was able to save Saul (Paul), we can have the assurance of salvation, "*Whoever will may come.*" Those who are able to take their position among the "whoever," have the assurance of salvation. Matthew took that place and was saved.

Jesus said, "*I have not come to call the righteous, but sinners to repentance*" (Luke 5:32). We need to be frequently reminded that Jesus came into the world to be our Saviour. "*You are to give him the name Jesus because he will save his people from their sins*" (Matthew 1:21).

If we believe ourselves to be righteous, Christ can do nothing for us, but if we consider ourselves to be among those who fail to reach the mark and are sinners, then Christ calls us to repentance. Jesus came into the world to save sinners and if we identify ourselves as one, then by trusting in Him, we too can know the joy of sins forgiven.

Matthew the Writer

Authorship

After the time of the Old Testament prophet Malachi, there followed 400 silent years. There was a falling away from God during this period. In Micah 5:2, we read of the prophecy of the place that Jesus the Christ would be born. Even Herod knew that this prophecy had been made, because he called his authorities and asked them about this prediction and where it had been prophesied that the Christ would be born. In Matthew chapter 2 verse l, we read of the fulfilment of this prophecy of Jesus birth.

Matthew's Gospel is therefore the bridge that leads us out of the Old Testament and into the New Testament. A Bible reader would be confused by the lack of information if he were to jump from Malachi into Mark, or Acts, or Romans. When Jesus was found healing the sick, Matthew said, "*This was to fulfil which was spoken through the prophet Isaiah*" (Matthew 8:17), demonstrating that the roots of the gospel are in the Old Testament and that the Gospel fulfils, completes and gives meaning to the Old Testament. The truth is further seen in Matthew's 53 Old Testament quotations and 76 references to Old Testament passages. Many of God's promises in the Old Testament are fulfilled in the New Testament.

Nowhere in the first Gospel is Matthew explicitly called its author, but the early writers of the church, who discussed the authorship, credit it to Matthew. The Didache - The Teaching of the Twelve Apostles - dated by most scholars to be between AD 80 – 100, is a brief early Christian treatise and has many quotes from Matthew's Gospel showing that this Gospel was used very early in the church.

Papias, Bishop of Hierapolis (c. AD 60-135) which was situated near Laodicea and Colossae in Asia Minor, presided over the Christians in the city. He claimed that "Matthew compiled the logia in the Hebrew tongue and everyone interpreted them as he was able." Logia means sayings or oracles and this might mean that Matthew made written records in Hebrew (or Aramaic) of our Lord's sayings – a list of His teachings - which were not then available in Greek and had to be translated on the spot by whoever used them.

Irenaeus (c. AD 115-202), Bishop of Lugdunum in Gaul, which is now Lyons, France, was a disciple of Polycarp, who himself was a disciple of John the Evangelist. He claimed that Matthew issued "a written gospel among the Hebrews in their own dialect, while Paul was preaching at Rome and laying the foundations of the church."

The scholar and early Christian theologian, Origen (c. AD 185-254) said, "Among the four Gospels which are the only indisputable ones in the Church of God under heaven, I have learned by tradition that the first is written according to Matthew, the same that was once a tax collector, but afterwards an emissary of Yeshua the Messiah, who having published it for the Jewish believers, wrote it in Hebrew."

Matthew, as a government official and tax-collector in Capernaum, would probably have been literate in both Greek and

Aramaic and accustomed to taking notes as a part of his business activity. Greek was the language used in the market-place.

Date of writing

It is unknown when the Gospel of Matthew was written but has been argued that it was written before the destruction of the Jewish temple in AD 70. This is significant because Jesus had prophesied concerning the temple when He said, "*Do you see all these things? I tell you the truth, not one stone here will be left on another; everyone will be thrown down*" (Matthew 24:2). This prophecy was fulfilled in AD 70 when the Romans sacked Jerusalem and burned the temple. It would be odd that no mention of its fulfilment would appear in the book had it been written after this date.

If Mark's Gospel was written first, as many scholars think, then the date of Mark's Gospel influences our choice of a date for Matthew. Irenaeus wrote that Mark composed his Gospel after Peter's death (about AD 64-67), during the Nero persecution. Nero was Roman emperor from AD 54 to 68. Clement of Alexandria said that Mark wrote his Gospel while Peter was still alive. The consensus among scholars is that the book of Mark was written between AD 50 and 60 and the book of Matthew was written between AD 60 and 70.

Purpose of Writing

The main purpose of Matthew's Gospel is to convince Jews everywhere that Jesus was the promised Messiah, the King and the Suffering Servant. He was accepted by God and rejected by the Jewish leaders and the nation of Israel.

Eusebius said Matthew wrote for his own countrymen. The writer speaks as one whose mind was full of the Old Testament Scriptures. He constantly saw prophecy fulfilled in our Lord and frequently quotes the Old Testament.

Matthew seems to have a two-fold purpose. He seeks to convince his Jewish readers that Jesus was in fact the promised Messiah. He quotes Messianic prophecies as being fulfilled in Jesus. The Jews looked for a Messianic King, and this Gospel greatly emphasised the coming of the Kingdom of God, through Jesus Christ, the King.

He seeks to record our Lord's teaching. Matthew gives us a number of our Lord's discourses in great detail. In fact we get the impression that these are the most important parts of the Gospel, and that the narrative portions which portray our Lord's actions have a secondary place. This is probably why Matthew does not always present his material in the order the events happened.

Matthew shows Christ to be the fulfilment of the Old Testament. In this Gospel more than any other we are told that something our Lord was or did is a fulfilment of an Old Testament prophecy – e.g. Matthew 1:22; 2:15; 3:3; 4:14; 12:17; 27:9. Note our Lord's own words in 5:17-18 where He says expressly that He had come not to destroy but to fulfil the law and the prophets.

Matthew preserves for us a very clear record of our Lord's teaching on spiritual principles of His Kingdom and on the kind of conduct required of those who would share in that Kingdom. Matthew records many parables which are introduced by the words "*The Kingdom of Heaven is like ......*"

Jesus, the Messiah King, is the major theme of Matthew. Matthew presents Jesus as the Christ, the King promised in the

Old Testament. He was offered to the Jews and rejected by them, crucified for those who believe, resurrected by God and now alive in heaven and is coming again.

Content

The former tax collector and bookkeeper was well able to trace the genealogy of Christ back through the royal line to David and then to Abraham, father of the Jews (Matthew 1:1). Matthew's ability with numbers shows up in the genealogy through his careful grouping of three sets of fourteen.

The Gospel of Matthew is filled with many references to Old Testament prophecies about the Messiah as being fulfilled in Jesus. Those quotations would have been of little interest to the Gentiles. But like the other apostles, Matthew eventually provoked the anger of the Jewish establishment and was forced to turn to the Gentiles who were willing to hear him.

The Gospel of Matthew is an excellent introduction to the central teachings of Christianity.

Matthew's intended audience was his fellow Jews, many of whom—especially the Pharisees and Sadducees—stubbornly refused to accept Jesus as their Messiah. In spite of centuries of reading and studying the Old Testament, their eyes were blinded to the truth of who Jesus was. Jesus rebuked them for their hard hearts and their refusal to recognize the One they had supposedly been waiting for (John 5:37-47). They wanted a Messiah on their own terms, one who would fulfil their own desires and do what they wanted Him to do.

Matthew records many of our Lord's discourses. We have the Sermon on the Mount, the Commission given to the disciples, the

Parables of chapter 13, the denunciations of the Pharisees and the discourses (and parables) relating to the consummation of the kingdom. It seems, as we have already noted, that Matthew was very anxious to leave a permanent and truly representative record of our Lord's work as a teacher.

Matthew uses the term *"the kingdom of heaven"* some 32 times. This Gospel also relates repentance to the kingdom. The idea of repentance is that God is King, the kingdom is the realm over which He rules and His subjects are to submit to Him.

The phrase *"the kingdom of heaven"* occurs only in the Gospel of Matthew and is used by both Jesus and John the Baptist, neither of whom explain the meaning of the term. This indicates that the Jews understood the meaning of the kingdom. The idea of kingship comes from the Old Testament. The kingdom of heaven is the rule and reign of God and His divine order on earth. In the New Testament the kingdom of heaven is past, present and future.

Matthew has many parables about the kingdom. In the parables he often says *"the kingdom of heaven is like"* and gives a parable to show similarities. The parables of the kingdom are designed to compel people to make a decision about who Jesus Christ is.

Matthew showed that Jesus is for all people and that His kingdom is for Gentiles as well as for Jews (Matthew 8:11; 12:50). Matthew is the only Synoptic Gospel which presents the church as the *"called out"* people of God. It is significant that Jesus presents this concept in response to Peter's Confession. It is also at this point that Jesus begins to teach His disciples about His death and resurrection.

Matthew places great emphasis on Jesus' teaching and groups them together. Matthew has great teachings about God and his central teaching is that God is gracious and loving. He refers to

Him as a father, and he does this more than anyone else in the New Testament. This is exceptional, since Matthew is writing primarily, though not exclusively, to Jewish people, and God as a father was not prominent in the Old Testament.

Although the Gospel of Matthew is strongly Jewish in character, it was written also for the benefit of Gentiles, since the final commission given to the twelve disciples was to *"Go and make disciples of all nations"* (Matthew 28:19).

The Life of Matthew after Jesus' Resurrection

Matthew was with the other disciples when they met in the upper room after Jesus' ascension when they chose Matthias to replace Judas Iscariot (Acts 1:13). They continued together until the day of Pentecost when the Holy Spirit came upon them.

An early tradition recounts that the apostles remained at Jerusalem for up to twelve years after the Ascension. Paul does not seem to have found any of the Apostles at Jerusalem when he met some of the Christian leaders in AD 56 (Acts 21:17). Nothing certain is known of Matthew's missionary labours. Like most of the apostles, Matthew seemed to have evangelized in a number of countries.

Tradition has it that after the dispersion of the apostles, Matthew travelled into Egypt and Ethiopia, preaching the Gospel. Parthia, Ethiopia, and India were believed to have been visited by Matthew. Irenaeus says he preached the Gospel among the Hebrews. Clement of Alexandria stated that Matthew spent fifteen years in this work. Eusebius records that Pantaenus discovered a copy of Matthew's Gospel in India, written in Hebrew. It was reported, "Bartholomew, one of the apostles, had preached to them, and left with them the writing of Matthew in the Hebrew language, which they had preserved till that time." It would be natural for a copy of Matthew's Gospel to have found its way to India if Matthew himself had been to India or to Persia. Persia was on the direct trade route from Antioch to India.

Matthew is believed to have remained in Egypt and Ethiopia for about twenty-three years but the manner of his death is uncertain; according to the Greek Legend he died in peace but, according to the tradition of the Western Church, he suffered martyrdom either by the sword or the spear.

There is disagreement as to whether or not he was martyred. According to some of the oldest sources, he was not martyred. Other sources hold that Ethiopia was the place where he died; and that he was stabbed to death there in the year AD 90 in the reign of Domitian.

Tradition has it that Matthew ministered to kings and high government officials. His former experience as an administrator may well have equipped him to witness to people in places of authority. Matthew was a gifted writer and perhaps the best educated of any of the twelve, and was well able to write the great Gospel which bears his name.

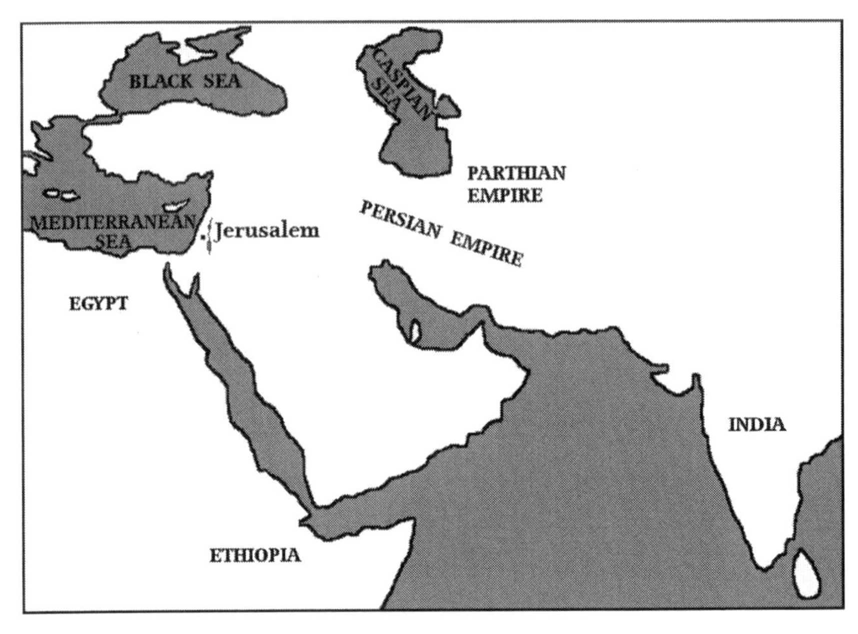

Map of places Matthew visited

Final comment

There is much we can learn from Matthew, even though we may not be able to identify with the extent of his early dishonesty and greed. We all face the challenge of accepting Christ and keeping Him at the centre of our lives. Jesus Christ wants all Christians to seek first His kingdom and His righteousness (Matthew 6:33). God can and does use people of all classes of society.

Matthew was a man of wealth and of economic security when Jesus called him, and he left it all to become a disciple. We know that material possessions can never fully satisfy us. Money, and the things it can buy, can make life more comfortable in this world, but it cannot fully and deeply satisfy the need of the soul.

The parable of the tax collector and the sinner in Luke 18:9-14 may well have been based on a real story. Jesus told His disciples about two men going to the temple to pray, one a Pharisee and the other a tax collector. The Pharisee prayed how good he was and fasted twice a week and was not like other people who were robbers and evildoers, whereas the tax collector, because of his reputation, stood at a distance, beat his breast and would not even look up to heaven.

However, notice what happened when Jesus called Matthew. His life was changed and, once Matthew made the choice and left his desk, he could not go back, nor did he ever regret making this decision. Matthew stands as a vivid reminder that the Lord often chooses the most despicable people of this world, redeems them and gives them new hearts, and uses them in remarkable ways.

When Jesus said to Matthew, *"Follow Me,"* Matthew knew there was in that command a promise of the forgiveness of his sin and he devoted the rest of his life to following Jesus.

Jesus said, *"It is not the healthy who need a doctor, but the sick. I have not come to call the righteous, but sinners to repentance"* (Luke 5:31-32). Jesus reserved His harshest words for the self-righteous, religious people who thought they had no need of mercy.

In conclusion, Matthew will ever remain an inspiration, as long as his Gospel is read. His transformed life is a reminder to each of us that we can also experience the power of Christ to change our lives, no matter the circumstances.

The apostle wrote all he knew about the Saviour so that his readers might experience in their lives Christ's power which is able to make them disciples. This is the individuality of the Gospel we must not lose.

JAMES
THE SON OF ALPHAEUS

(Matthew 10:3; Mark 3:18; Luke 6:15 and Acts 1:13)

James, son of Alphaeus, was one of the twelve disciples of Jesus Christ. He is mentioned under this name only four times in the New Testament in all three Synoptic Gospels and in Acts; each time in the list of the twelve disciples. However, according to the translation used in the Gospel of Mark, he is also identified as "the minor," "the little," "the less," or "the younger" (Mark 15:40). He is also mentioned twice in connection with his mother, "Mary the mother of James" (Mark 16:1; Luke 24:10).

The title, "the younger" or "the less," is used to distinguish James from the other disciple named James. Since it means that he is either younger or smaller in size, he seems to be compared to one other James. In the lists of the twelve apostles, there are two apostles called James who are identified by their fathers: James, son of Zebedee, and James, son of Alphaeus. Since James, son of Alphaeus is called "James the less," it has been claimed that the other James, James the son of Zebedee, is sometimes called "James the greater." This James was part of Jesus' inner circle of three and the first disciple to be martyred.

A third James appears in the New Testament. He was the half-brother of the Lord Jesus (Mark 6:3), a leader in the Jerusalem church, and writer of the book of James. He was not one of the early disciples for we are told that Jesus' brothers did not believe in Him (John 7:5; Mark 3:21).

We are told that James was the son of Alphaeus, but in Mark 2:14 we are told that Jesus called the tax collector Levi, son of Alphaeus. This leads some people to conclude that James and Levi (Matthew) were brothers. However, the four times that James, son of Alphaeus, is mentioned directly in the Bible (each time in the list of the apostles) the only family relationship stated is that his father was Alphaeus. Matthew and James are never linked together and referred to as brothers, whereas Peter and Andrew; James (a different James) and John, were consistently referred to as being brothers. However, had these things been of significant importance, scripture would have revealed them to us.

James becomes a Disciple

We do not know how or when James, the son of Alphaeus, followed Jesus. We are told that Jesus called James and John, the sons of Zebedee, when they were preparing their fishing nets (Mark1:19); Andrew brought his brother Simon to Jesus (John 1:41-42); as Jesus was leaving for Galilee He found Philip and called him (John 1:43); Philip brought Nathanael to Jesus (John 1:45-46), and Matthew was sitting at his tax collector's booth when Jesus called him (Matthew 9:9).

We are not told in scripture how James became a disciple. We do not even know what type of work he was involved in before he was "called." All we know is that he became one of the privileged Twelve, but never more than a name on the list.

In Mark's Gospel we read that when Jesus was crucified, several women stood at a distance looking on, including Mary Magdalene and Mary the mother of James the younger. We are told that these women had followed Jesus when he was in Galilee and had *"cared for his needs"* there (Mark 15:40-41). From this information, we know that James had the advantage of a mother who followed Jesus and lived in a godly home. We are not told if James's mother led him to Jesus or if James led his mother to Jesus.

Some of the memorable mothers of the Bible are Sarah, the wife of Abraham, mother of Isaac, the son of promise (Genesis 21:1-7); Hannah, wife of Elkanah, mother of Samuel, the noteworthy prophet of God (1 Samuel 1:1-28); Elizabeth, wife of Zechariah the priest, mother of John the Baptist (Luke 1:57-66); Mary, wife of Joseph, mother of Jesus Christ (Luke 2:1-52), and Eunice, the wife of a Greek and mother of Timothy, the young helper for the Apostle Paul (Acts 16:1; 2 Timothy 1:5). What an amazing privilege to have a godly mother and her influence on the family!

This is contrasted with the influence of a bad mother. The evil influence of Jezebel on her husband, Ahab, is seen in 1 Kings 21:1-16 and caused the death of Naboth and the loss of his vineyard. This was the start of a wicked dynasty for we are told, "*Ahaziah was twenty-two years old when he became king and he reigned in Jerusalem for one year. His mother's name was Athaliah, a granddaughter of Omri. He too walked in the ways of the house of Ahab, for his mother encouraged him in doing wrong. He did evil in the eyes of the Lord, as the house of Ahab had done*" (2 Chronicles 22:2-4). What a tragedy for a mother to lead her family in doing wrong! A child can have no greater privilege than to have parents who will seek to show their children to the Saviour and experience the joy of the Christian life.

Parents who want to give their children the best in life are tempted to give them money, guidance for a career and leave them an inheritance, but the greatest gift is the influence towards a living faith in Christ. Jesus said, "*What good is it for a man to gain the whole world, yet forfeit his soul?*" (Mark 8:36)

So, whatever else James may not have had, he had a mother who followed Christ, and perhaps a father of the same conviction. He heard the call of Jesus and became a member of Jesus' group and one day his name, with the names of the other apostles, will be written on the twelve foundations of the wall of the Holy City, Jerusalem (Revelation 21:14).

James the Disciple

The Bible tells us so little about James the younger that we might sum up the information in a paragraph. We have no record of the things he said or the places where he worked. Scripture is silent about the places he went with Jesus and the other disciples. He displayed no great leadership qualities and asked no searching questions, but this does not mean that he was inactive or that he was ineffective.

On the contrary, we have every reason to assume that James, the son of Alphaeus, was as busy as any of the other disciples, preaching, teaching, healing the sick, and blessing others as he had been blessed. He had a low profile among the Twelve. Perhaps his uniqueness was the fact that so much about him is unknown. The Lord chose him for a purpose, mentored and trained him like the others, and sent him out as a witness.

James must have gone about his work without drawing attention to himself and is an example of all those who quietly go about their work and are soon forgotten in spite of their great efforts and accomplishments. These are the people who usually show up to help when there is a job to be done, or someone in need, without asking for anything in return.

It is encouraging that James was included in the list of Jesus' disciples, to represent the silent majority of people who do not seek recognition or appreciation for their work. We should remember God judges us, not on the basis of how much we achieve, but on the basis of how much we do with the gifts and talents we have been given.

The parable in Matthew 25:14-30 tells of a master who left his home to travel and, before leaving, entrusted his property to his servants (property worth eight talents – a talent was a large unit of money). One servant received five talents, the second two talents, and the third one talent, according to their respective abilities.

Returning after a long absence, the master asked his servants for an account of how they used the talents given to them. The first two servants explained that they had each put their money to work and doubled its value, and so they were rewarded accordingly. The third servant, however, had merely hidden his talent in a hole in the ground, and was punished for his failure to use his talent wisely.

Traditionally, the parable of the talents has been seen as an exhortation to Jesus' disciples to use their God-given gifts in the service of God, and to take risks for the sake of the Kingdom of God. These gifts have been seen to include personal abilities ("talents" in the everyday sense), as well as personal wealth. Failure to use one's gifts, the parable suggests, will result in judgement. We don't know what gifts James had and used but, whatever they were, apparently our Lord considered them adequate and right for James.

On one occasion, Jesus saw rich people putting money into the temple treasury and a poor widow putting in her two very small copper coins. Jesus said, "*This poor widow has put in more than all the others. All these people gave their gifts out of their wealth, but she out of her poverty put in all she had to live on*" (Luke 21:3-4).

Here we learn that everything we do is seen by Jesus Christ and that those who give all to Him will be rewarded no matter how small their efforts may be. Even though the labours of James are not recorded in scripture, they will not go unrewarded. Unseen, loving and devoted labour for Jesus Christ is never overlooked or forgotten in heaven.

Mordecai uncovered a conspiracy plot to assassinate King Xerxes and the guilty people were executed. However, he received no credit for it. Mordecai may have thought with the passing of years that his deed would never be known. But one sleepless night, the king learned from reading the historical records that Mordecai had not only saved his life but had gone unrewarded. The result was that the king appointed him to the position of prime minister (Esther 2:19-23; 6:1-10).

The names of the Magi who searched for Jesus are unknown (Matthew 2:7-12). We do not know the name of the boy who gave his lunch to Jesus to feed the 5,000 people (John 6:9); or the man who provided the donkey on which Jesus rode into Jerusalem (Luke 19:33-34); or the man who made available his guest room for the Last Supper (Mark 14:14-15).

Many good deeds may go unnoticed and without public recognition or be kept secret on purpose. Those who speak highly of their own achievements may receive the praise of men, but those who quietly go about their work will one day receive recognition and the praise of our heavenly Master. God will not forget what we do. If we should only give a cup of water to those in need, we will receive our reward (Matthew 10:42).

Some scholars draw our attention to the fact that James, son of Alphaeus, is always listed in the last group of four apostles:

In Matthew we have, "James son of Alphaeus, and Thaddaeus, Simon the Zealot and Judas Iscariot" (Matthew 10:3).

In Mark we have, "James son of Alphaeus, Thaddaeus, Simon the Zealot and Judas Iscariot" (Mark 3:18-19).

In Luke we have, "James son of Alphaeus, Simon who was called the Zealot, Judas son of James (Thaddaeus), and Judas Iscariot" (Luke 6: 15-16).

They suggest that the last three, Thaddaeus, Simon the Zealot and Judas Iscariot may have had links with the Zealot Party. The Zealots were a group of revolutionaries who hated the Romans and were struggling to free Jerusalem from Roman occupation. They opposed the payment of tribute by Israel to a pagan emperor on the ground that this was treason to God, Israel's true King. If that is true, we may speculate that James, son of Alphaeus, could have been included here because he too had association with the Zealot party.

The other interesting thing is that if James, son of Alphaeus, had leanings towards the Zealot Party and if he and Matthew, who was a tax collector for the Roman occupation forces, were brothers, it shows how two sons could be brought up in the same home and yet chose completely different paths in life. It also shows that Jesus brought into His group of twelve disciples, people of very different opinions and resolved the possible ensuing conflicts by changing their lives. Alphaeus' family could have been a divided family because Matthew had become a tax collector and supported Rome. James and Matthew must have been reconciled to one another by Jesus.

James, son of Alphaeus, after Pentecost

Little is known concerning what James, son of Alphaeus, did after Pentecost. Some of the earliest traditions about him say that he took the gospel to Syria and Persia. Accounts differ concerning how he died, some say he was stoned and others say he was beaten to death. Others say he was stoned to death by the Jews, and was buried beside the temple. Another tradition maintains he was crucified at Ostrakine in Lower Egypt where he had been preaching the gospel.

It is claimed that the body of James, the son of Alphaeus, was taken from Jerusalem to Constantinople, and then it was taken from Constantinople to Rome about the year 572 and was interred by Pope John III in the Church of the Holy Apostles.

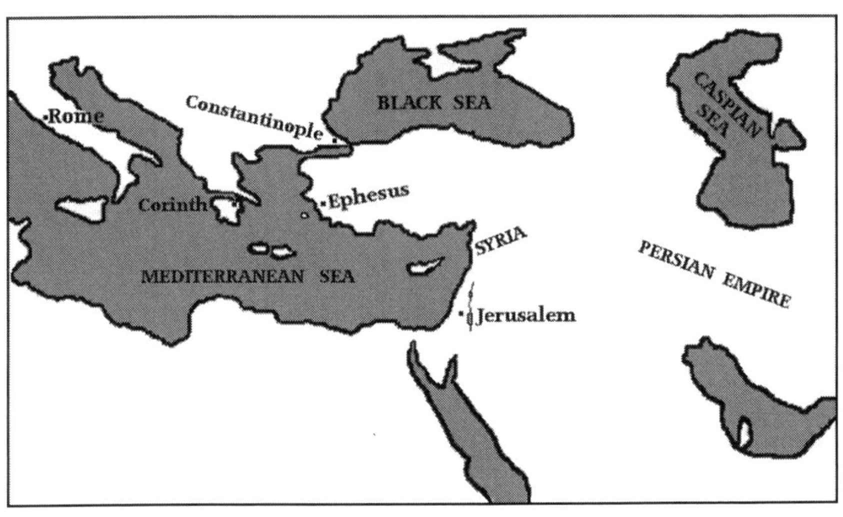

Map of Places of places James son of Alphaeus visited

Even though the world remembers almost nothing about James, the son of Alphaeus, in eternity he will receive a full reward. He will always have the honour and distinction of having been chosen by Jesus to be His apostle. The apostle James demonstrates to us that it is not the worker who is important in the kingdom of God. This is why the apostle Paul rebuked those causing the division in the Corinthian church when some said they followed Paul and others Apollos. Paul said, "*What, after all, is Apollos?*

And what is Paul? Only servants ....neither he who plants nor he who waters is anything, but only God, who makes things grow" (1 Corinthians 3:3-9).

Maybe we feel that we are not important in the church and think that we have no special talents. Don't forget that God knows everyone and sees everything we do. He will reward us if we are faithful.

Thaddeus
the Disciple with Three Names

Like James the son of Alphaeus, little is known about Thaddaeus, another of the twelve disciples, and we are not sure what name to call him. Bible scholars generally agree that he is known by three different names in scripture.

The first three Gospels mention him in the list of apostles. Some versions of Matthew refer to him as *"Lebbaeus, whose surname was Thaddaeus"* (Matthew 10:3 KJV). Mark called him Thaddaeus (Mark 3:18). The King James Version of Luke 6:16 calls him Judas *"the brother of James,"* while later versions change this phrase to *"the son of James."* The original text contains neither "son" nor "brother" but *"Judas of James."* When names are connected in this way, it usually means the first person is a son of the second. John identified him as *"Judas not Judas Iscariot"* (John 14:22). Luke also called him *"Judas son of James"* in Acts 1:13. Comparison of lists shows these three names referred to the same person.

There are several men in the New Testament who are called James. There is James, son of Mary and half-brother of Jesus; James, son of Zebedee and brother of the apostle John; and James son of Alphaeus, also known as James the younger. It is however also possible that James, the father of Thaddaeus was someone not identified in the New Testament. We have no definite proof about the background of Thaddaeus, except that he was related to someone called James.

The issue is further confused when he is identified by some scholars as the author of the epistle of Jude. However, the author claims to be *"Jude, a servant of Jesus Christ and brother of James"* (Jude 1), this would make him the half brother of our Lord Jesus Christ (see Mark 6:3). However, since none of our Lord's brothers believed in Him during His earthly ministry, Judas could not have been one of the early disciples (John 7:5). In fact, the author of Jude places himself out of the circle of the apostles when he speaks of them as "they" instead of "we" (Jude 17-18).

Some scholars have the view that Thaddaeus and Lebbaeus are simply different versions of the same name. On the other hand, we could say it was not unusual for a person to have three names at that time, just as it is not unusual for children to be given several names today. So it is possible that this man's full name was Judas Lebbaeus Thaddaeus, and that he was known by all three of those names.

Therefore, it is possible that he was called Judas by his family in the early years of his life, but after Jesus was crucified, he introduced himself as 'Judas, but I am not Iscariot.' Later he may have decided it was much easier to introduce himself as Thaddaeus and his friends also called him by that name. Both Matthew and Mark called him "Thaddaeus" (Matt. 10:3; Mark 3:18). When John mentioned him by the name Judas, he added "not Iscariot" (John 14:22).

Thaddaeus asks a Question
(John 14:22)

We do not know how and when Thaddaeus became a disciple, all we have is his name included in the list of disciples. In all lists of the disciples in the Gospels, Peter, Andrew, James, and John are always the first four names and James son of Alphaeus, Thaddaeus, Simon the Zealot and Judas Iscariot are always the last four names. It has been suggested that these four were grouped together last because all of them were associated with the Zealot Movement.

If Thaddaeus was associated with the Zealot Movement, he would have wanted Jesus to make a public demonstration of power and mount a full-scale campaign against Rome. If Thaddaeus really was a Zealot, he may have been confused and disappointed by what he saw as Jesus' apparent lack of action.

Near the end of Jesus' ministry on this earth, He gathered His disciples together to tell them that He would soon be leaving to prepare a place for them. This caused a number of questions to be asked by His disciples.

Thomas asked the question *"Lord, we don't know where you are going, so how can we know the way"* (John 14:5). Jesus then explained to them that He was the way, but this raised another question from Philip, who said, *"Lord, show us the Father and that will be enough for us"* (John 14:8). This caused further discussion when Jesus promised that He would send the Holy Spirit to be with them.

Jesus was teaching the disciples that the Holy Spirit would come as the Comforter to be with His people at all times. Jesus would be physically leaving this world and the disciples would not see Him again. Jesus told them, *"Before long, the world will not see me anymore, but you will see me. Because I live, you also will live . . . . He who loves me will be loved by my Father, and I too will love him and show myself to him*" (John 14:19, 21). The Holy Spirit will be with those who trust Jesus as their Saviour.

Perhaps Judas Thaddaeus did not understand what Jesus meant and was getting impatient, wanting Jesus to reveal Himself as soon as possible and asked, "*Lord, why do you intend to show yourself to us and not to the world?*" (John 14:22). This was the only question, and the only statement, ever recorded that Judas Thaddaeus made.

This question is asked by one seeking after the truth, and not able to see clearly what our Lord's words meant – whether a visible or an invisible revelation of Himself. Following the other questions asked by Peter, Thomas and Philip about seeing the Father and in a little while seeing Jesus no more, Judas Thaddaeus focused on the physical presence rather than the spiritual.

The answer Jesus gave could easily have disappointed him still more. "*If anyone loves me, he will obey my teaching. My Father will love him, and we will come to him and make our home with him*" (John 14:23).

Thaddaeus wanted to know why Jesus wasn't going to make Himself known to everyone. He was obviously still hoping to see the kingdom come to earth. Of course that is how Jesus taught His disciples to pray (Luke 11:2). Christ would show Himself to anyone who loves Him. Thaddaeus was in effect asking why Jesus had not taken over and shown Himself to the world.

When Jesus said "*Because I live, you also will live,*" Thaddaeus was confused and this prompted him to ask his question regarding Jesus showing Himself to the disciples and not to the world. Jesus was saying that the life of the Christian is secure and can never be destroyed. He or she has everlasting life now, and in heaven after death, because Jesus Christ our Saviour lives.

Jesus went on to explain that the Holy Spirit, whom the Father would send, would remind them of everything He had taught them. Jesus had taught the disciples many things while He was physically with them.

The promised Holy Spirit gives us comfort. When we are distressed - God is there. When we are depressed - God is there. He is an ever-present help in time of trouble. He will never leave us - nor forsake us. His love is always pointed in our direction. Paul said, "*For I am convinced that neither death nor life, neither angels nor demons, neither the present nor the future, nor any powers, neither height nor depth, nor anything else in all creation, will be able to separate us from the love of God that is in Christ Jesus our Lord*" (Romans 8:38-39).

With Thaddaeus asking his question, we have been given this wonderful explanation and comfort of knowing that the Holy Spirit will be with us at all times.

Thaddaeus after Pentecost

After Jesus' crucifixion and resurrection, He appeared to His disciples over a period of forty days "*and gave many convincing proofs that He was alive*" (Acts 1:3). Jesus then ascended from Mount of Olives back to heaven with the disciples watching. The disciples returned to Jerusalem to the upper room where they were staying and Thaddaeus (Judas son of James) was with them (Acts 1:13).

Thaddaeus continued to be with the disciples while they chose Matthias to replace Judas Iscariot and also when the Holy

Spirit descended upon them on the day of Pentecost. It appears that he finally came to understand the answer Jesus gave him because, according to Christian legend, Thaddaeus spent the rest of his life preaching the gospel in Judea, Samaria, Idumea, Syria, Mesopotamia, and Libya. Most of the early traditions suggest that a few years after Pentecost, he took the gospel north to Edessa, a royal city in Mesopotamia, in the region of Turkey today.

The ancient city-state of Edessa was situated between the River Euphrates and the River Tigris, rivers in the upper Mesopotamian Fertile Crescent. It was important in that a major trade route between Europe and the Middle East ran through it. The capital Edessa overlooked a passage crucial to the trade route. Today, the city is called Şanliurfa or simply Urfa and is located in south eastern Turkey near the border with Iraq. As with northern Iraq, most of the population today is Kurdish, though there are many Arabs and Turks in the city as well. The main religion today is Muslim but there are also Christian and Jewish minorities. According to local tradition and the belief of some Muslims, Urfa was the Biblical city of Ur, the birthplace of Abraham.

There are a number of ancient accounts of how Thaddaeus brought about a miraculous healing for King Abgar V of Edessa, in Mesopotamia, which resulted in the king's conversion to Christianity. Eusebius, the historian, said the archives at Edessa (now destroyed) contained full records of Thaddaeus's visit and the healing of Abgar, who had been gravely ill.

The Apostles Bartholomew and Thaddaeus are traditionally believed to have been the first to take Christianity to Armenia where many people were converted and secret Christian communities established. They are, therefore, honoured as the patron saints of the Armenian Apostolic Church. The Saint Bartholomew Monastery (now in south eastern Turkey) and the Saint Thaddaeus

Monastery (now in northern Iran) were established as a result. They were both built in what was then Armenia. Armenia became the first Christian nation in the world. Christianity was officially proclaimed in AD 301 as the national religion of Armenia.

Armenians cling to the belief that Qara Kelisa is the world's first church and was first built on the present site in AD 68 in memory of Saint Thaddaeus. In AD 45 he had travelled to Armenia, then part of the Persian Empire, to preach about Jesus Christ. On several occasions the church was destroyed by invasions from neighbouring countries and struck by earthquakes. It was destroyed as a result of an earthquake in 1319 and rehabilitated in 1329. The church was repaired in 1691 with black stones and in 1810 with white stones and further renewed and enlarged during the course of the following centuries.

Qara Kelisa has specific Armenian architecture and is considered one of the most valuable historical monuments of the country in terms of technique and volume. The location of the monastery was obviously carefully chosen, for it was built during a period when it was under serious threat by the neighbouring peoples. The thick walls around the monastery also had an important protective purpose during sieges, and the impressive building was built especially to withstand them. The building is world famous and a great number of Armenians from inside and outside the country come to the church to hold religious rituals.

There is a church in Iran in the northern province of West Azerbaijan which is called Qara Kelisa and also known as the St.Thaddaeus Church. Annually at this church, on the week beginning July 22, a ceremony is held to honour the memory of Saint Thaddaeus.

Large numbers of Armenians, Assyrians and Catholics from Iran and other countries attend as part of their pilgrimage on the

Day of St. Thaddaeus. The ceremony is one of the largest religious ceremonies held by Armenians. Qara Kelisa is one of the oldest and most famous surviving Christian monuments of Iran and carries great significance for the country's Armenian Orthodox community.

There are several traditions concerning Thaddaeus. One tradition states that he evangelised in Syria and northern Persia and that he died there and was originally buried at Qara Kelisa. Later it is possible that a part, or all of his body, was removed to Rome and Tolosa, Spain. According to other traditions, Thaddaeus suffered martyrdom about AD 65 in Beirut in the Roman province of Syria, together with the apostle Simon the Zealot, after years devoted to bringing others to Jesus. Sometime after his death, his body was taken from Beirut to Rome and placed in a crypt in St. Peter's Basilica. Another tradition states that his remains were preserved in an Armenian monastery on an island in the northern part of Kyrgyzstan at least until the mid-15th century. Later legends either deny that the remains are preserved there or claim that they were moved to a more desolate stronghold in the Pamir Mountains.

The traditional apostolic symbol of Judas Lebbaeus Thaddaeus is a club, because tradition says he was clubbed to death for his faith. Fox's Book of Martyrs records that Thaddaeus or Jude was crucified for his faith at Edessa in AD 72. Others believe that he was pierced with arrows when he refused to deny his faith in Christ. Regardless of the method, it is commonly accepted that he was martyred for his faith in Christ.

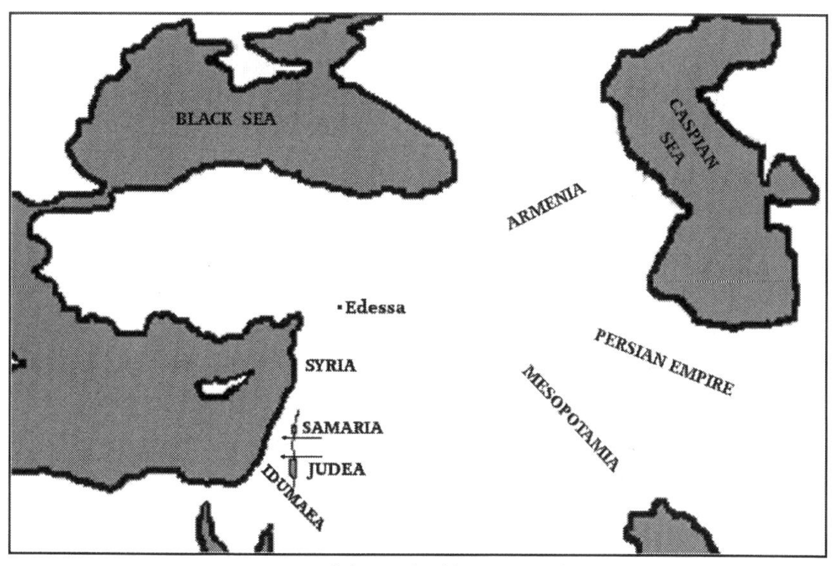

Map of places Thaddaeus visited

Thaddaeus will receive His Reward

Thaddaeus was a disciple that very little is known about but one day he will receive his reward. What a tragedy it will be in the final day that there will be people whose names may be well known in society and listed among the rich and famous but their names will be missing from the Book of Life. They will have had their reward on earth but will spend eternity separated from Jesus Christ because they did not receive the free gift of salvation that He offered them (Eph. 2:8-9).

Whereas, there will be others like Thaddaeus, who will not leave behind any record of great accomplishments on earth but hear the most important words anyone could ever hear from Jesus, "*Well done, good and faithful servant*!" (Matt. 25:21)

For whatever reason, we do not have an in depth record of Thaddaeus's service as a disciple of Christ. The fact that he is named among the Twelve shows us he was important to Jesus. At this point in Jesus' ministry, there were many people following Jesus everywhere He went. Out of this great number of followers Jesus only selected twelve. Thaddaeus was privileged to be called to be in that number.

Though we do not know anything of Thaddaeus's life, we are certain that like Peter, James, John, Andrew and Levi, he left everything he had in order to follow Jesus. Notice a conversation between Peter and Jesus on the subject of rewards. Peter's comment was, *"We have left everything to follow you! What then will there be for us?"* Jesus said to them, *"I tell you the truth, at the renewal of all things, when the Son of Man will sit on his glorious throne, you who have followed me will also sit on twelve thrones, judging the twelve tribes of Israel"* (Matthew 19:27-28).

Though the world may not recognize your effort, though you may never be "rewarded" in this life, Jesus has much more waiting for you. You will have an eternal reward! *"Do not store up for yourselves treasures on earth, where moth and rust destroy, and where thieves break in and steal. But store up for yourselves treasures in heaven, where moth and rust do not destroy, and where thieves do not break in and steal"* (Matthew 6:19-20).

We may not know many details of Thaddaeus's story but he will have treasures in heaven and, as a result, receive his reward for being a faithful servant. The world may not know your name, realize your worth, or recognize your effort ....BUT JESUS DOES!

SIMON
THE ZEALOT

Matthew 10:4; Mark 3:18; Luke 6:15 and Acts 1:13

Two men called Simon are listed among the twelve disciples. There is the well known Simon Peter, and there is Simon the Zealot who is not so well known. We have many stories about Simon Peter, the things he said and the work he was involved in, but for Simon the Zealot there are only four references to him in scripture: Matthew 10:4; Mark 3:18; Luke 6:15 and Acts 1:13. On each occasion, he is mentioned with the names of the other apostles. Unlike Simon Peter, not a single word or deed Simon the Zealot ever said or did has been recorded for us.

It is interesting to note that he is recorded in tenth place in the names listed in Luke and Acts and eleventh in Matthew and Mark. Since Judas Iscariot, the traitor, was always in twelfth position, that makes Simon the Zealot near the last in each list of the twelve apostles.

In Matthew 10:4 and Mark 3:18 he is called *"Simon the Canaanite"* (KJV) or "the Cananaean" (RSV and ESV). This is not a reference to the land of Canaan. The word *'kananaios'* is an Aramaic word which means "to be zealous" and is the exact Hebrew equivalent of the word for Zealot. In Luke 6:15 he is called, *"Simon, who was called the Zealot"* (NIV, RSV, ESV) and in Acts 1:13 he is called, *"Simon the Zealot"* (RSV, ESV).

Scripture does not tell us when or how he met Christ. All that is recorded of Simon is his name and that he was "a Zealot." A fact to be remembered is that after Christ chose Simon as an apostle, he never ceased to be known as "the Zealot." This may suggest that he was a member of an organisation called the Zealots. The Zealots were the political, violently anti-Roman wing of the Pharisees.

Jews divided into four religious parties

Josephus, the early church historian, speaks of "four schools of thought," or "four sects," into which the Jews were divided at that time.

i) The Pharisees who controlled and dominated the religious lives of the Jewish people were the "conservative party" within Judaism. Their name comes from the Hebrew root that can mean "to separate," so they may have sought purity by separating themselves from anything unclean. They considered themselves to be the only ones who could interpret scripture correctly. To disagree with them was to risk severe penalties, even imprisonment, torture and death. The torture and crucifixion of Jesus shows the hatred the Pharisees had for the Truth which was at odds with their doctrines. They frequently caused abuse and ridicule to Jesus.

They hypocritically despised all those who did not meet their standard of law-keeping. On many occasions, Jesus said, "*Woe to you, teachers of the law and Pharisees, you hypocrites!*" Usually the Pharisees were vehemently opposed to the Sadducees.

ii) The Sadducees were active in Judea from the second century BC until the destruction of the Temple in AD 70. They .were elitists who wanted to maintain the priestly caste, but they were also liberal in their willingness to incorporate Hellenism into their lives. (The Hellenistic period was the period of ancient Greek and

Mediterranean history between the death of Alexander the Great in 323 BC, and the emergence of the Roman Empire as signified by the Battle of Actium in 31 BC. During this period Greek culture flourished, spreading through the Mediterranean and into the Near East and Asia). This was something the Pharisees opposed. The Sadducees were generally wealthy members of the Jewish aristocracy and were popular among the high-class minority. They did not believe in an afterlife, "*The Sadducees say that there is no resurrection, and that there are neither angels nor spirits, but the Pharisees acknowledge them all*" (Acts 23:8).

The main difference between the Sadducees and the Pharisees is the interpretation of the Law of Moses (the first five books of the Bible called the *Torah*). The Sadducees stressed the need to live according to the commandments in the written Law. The Pharisees taught that the written Law had been given to the Jews and therefore, they were free to interpret it.

As a consequence, the Pharisees said that the 'written Torah' was to be supplemented with 'the oral Torah', the interpretation of the written Law by the rabbis – the Pharisee teachers. The Sadducees considered this an almost blasphemous act because it seemed to deny the majesty of the Law of Moses. The Sadducees seemed to disappear around AD 70, after the destruction of the Second Temple.

iii) The Essenes were the third religious party or sect, who emerged out of disgust with the other two. They are not mentioned in scripture, but Josephus and Philo make reference to them. This sect believed the others had corrupted the city and the Temple. They moved out of Jerusalem and lived a monastic life in the desert, devoting their lives to the study of the Law and adopting strict dietary laws and a commitment to celibacy.

Josephus records that the Essenes existed in large numbers

and thousands lived throughout Roman Judea. They practised the seventh day Sabbath and believed in reincarnation, also non-violence to all living creatures and the sharing of all material possessions. They were not involved in the politics of the Sadducees and Pharisees and shunned publicity.

iv) **The Zealots** were the fourth religious party or sect. The early historian Josephus calls them the 'dagger-men,' because they would not hesitate to drive a dagger into the heart of a Roman who came across their path. Their motto was, "We have no King but God." They were men of intense dedication and violent passion and were frequently involved in the assassination of Roman soldiers and officials.

The Zealots were a group of revolutionaries who hated the Romans and struggled to free Jerusalem from Roman occupation. They opposed the payment of tribute by Israel to a pagan emperor on the ground that this was treason to God, Israel's true King.

The decline and break-up of Israel as a nation

Between 1050 and 1000 BC, under King David, Israel came to its political zenith in the whole Mediterranean basin, from the Nile to the Euphrates. This was at a time when Egypt, Syria and Babylon were all weak. After David's death, Solomon became king and initially had a very successful reign. However, later in his reign, according to 1 Kings 11:30-34, the Lord would punish Solomon because of his sins, and the people forsaking God and worshipping false gods. (This would take place after Solomon's death, by removing ten of the twelve Tribes of Israel from his kingdom).

After Solomon's death, ten of the Tribes of Israel refused to accept Solomon's son Rehoboam as king, causing the united monarchy to split. The northern kingdom of Israel, consisting of ten tribes, were then ruled by Jeroboam, the son of Nebat, a member of the Tribe of Ephraim; while Rehoboam continued to reign in the southern kingdom of Judah, consisting of the remaining two tribes.

This, however, became the start of the decline of power and influence of Israel as a nation. In 721 BC, the Assyrian army captured the Israelite capital, Samaria, and carried away the citizens of the northern ten tribes. In 621 BC the capital and heart of the Assyrian Empire was destroyed by Babylonian and Median armies, effectively ending the Assyrian Empire. Later in 586 BC, the Babylonians completely defeated the southern kingdom of Israel – the remaining two tribes.

The rise of an opposition force

Seleucus established himself in Babylon in 312 BC, the year used as the foundation date of the Seleucid Empire. He ruled not only Babylon, but the entire enormous eastern part of Alexander's empire. The Seleucid kings were particularly cruel. When Antiochus became ruler of the Seleucid Empire, he was insensitive to the views of religious Jews. He did everything in his power to antagonize them, including erecting a pagan altar to Zeus over the altar of Yahweh. Jews who would not renounce their religious faith and accept the Greek idols and forms of worship were murdered on the spot. Observing the Sabbath and circumcision were forbidden on penalty of death.

In 167 BC, Antiochus sent some of his officers to the village of Modein to force the Jews living there to offer sacrifices to the pagan gods. Mattathias, as a leader in the city, was commanded by the officers to be the first person to offer a sacrifice, as an example to the rest of the people. He refused with a noble speech reminiscent of the words of Joshua in Joshua 24:14-15 (see: I Maccabees 2:15-22).

Because Mattathias refused, and fearing bloody reprisals against the people for his refusal, a certain Jew stepped forward and volunteered to offer the sacrifices to the pagan gods in the place of this aged priest. At this point, Mattathias was so overcome with a passionate zeal to defend his God that he killed this Jewish man, as well as the officers of the king. He then tore down the altar to the pagan gods and ran through the village shouting, "Let everyone who is zealous for the Law and who stands by the covenant follow me!" (I Maccabees 2:27). Mattathias and his five sons, who were all priests, and ministered in the Temple at Jerusalem, fled with a good number of followers to the mountains of the Judean wilderness.

These men, who became known as the Maccabees, organized themselves into a large, powerful guerrilla army. They soon began to launch raids against the towns and villages of the land, tearing down the pagan altars, killing the officials of Antiochus, and executing those Jews who were worshipping the pagan gods. The aged priest, Mattathias, was much too old for such a rigorous lifestyle, and died in 166 BC just as the rebellion was gaining momentum. As the father was dying, he said to his sons, "Be zealous with the law, and do not hesitate to give your life for the holy cause." This fostered in them an attitude that prompted the beginning of the Zealot Movement.

After much fighting, Judas, who succeeded his father as leader, decided to enter Jerusalem, liberate the city, purify the Temple and rededicate it to God. After he achieved the liberation of Jerusalem and the restoration of their religious practices in the Temple, Judas and his rebels turned their attention to the task of seeking to liberate all of Palestine from pagan control. Within a brief period of time, they were able to regain possession of much of the land.

However, their successes were short-lived for, in 160 BC, Lysias, the successor to Antiochus, raised a large army against them. Judas was killed and only a few of his followers escaped into the wilderness.

In the years to follow, conflict continued sporadically. After the death of Simon in 135 BC, the last of the sons of the aged priest Mattathias, the heroic period of Jewish history known as the Maccabean Revolt, came to an end.

The Zealot underground Movement

In 63 BC, the Roman general Pompey conquered Palestine, and brought it into the Roman Empire. In 51 BC, civil war broke out in the Roman Empire between Pompey, the party supporting the senate, and Julius Caesar and his supporters. About 45 BC, a Jewish patriot named Ezekias (Hezekiah), from Trachonitis (east of Galilee), led a band of freedom fighters against the Romans and their supporters. Herod became governor of Galilee and acted quickly to capture and execute the outlaw Ezekias and most of his followers.

The Jewish aristocracy in Jerusalem complained to Hyrcanus II, high priest from about 79 to 40 BC that Herod had acted contrary to Jewish Law by executing Ezekias and his supporters, and demanded that Herod be brought to trial for murder before the Sanhedrin. When he showed up, he appeared as a king, dressed in purple and attended by his bodyguard. Sextus Caesar, the governor of Syria, gave the orders to Hyrcanus that Herod should be acquitted or there would be great consequences and as a result the Sanhedrin freed him. By 37 BC, when Herod seized power, many people had lost their lives because of him.

Herod died in 4 BC, and his kingdom was divided among

his sons, who became tetrarchs ("rulers of a quarter part"). One of these quarters was Judea, corresponding to the region of the ancient Kingdom of Judah. Herod's son, Herod Archelaus, ruled Judea so badly that he was dismissed in AD 6 by the Roman Emperor Augustus, after an appeal from his own citizens.

In AD 6, Judea was officially incorporated into the Roman Empire and thus the state of Israel as an independent nation stopped. A census was ordered, and Quirinius, governor of Syria, carried out this order so that the new province could be appropriately taxed.

The priests in Jerusalem urged restraint and cooperation with the Romans; but Hezekiah's son, Judah, urged violent resistance. A popular Pharisee named Zadok, also from Galilee, supported Judah. These men did not get far in opposing the power of Rome, but they started something which gave rise to the re-emergence of the Zealot party. They saw the census and the new taxes as a subtle plot by the Roman occupation. The Zealots were afraid that this new tax would strike at the root of the established religion, by drawing off revenue that would otherwise be used in support of the Temple.

The Zealots developed into an underground movement, capable of sabotage and murder. They were patriots who swore on their life that they would resist Roman rule at all costs. It is thought that Barabbas, the prisoner charged with murder and insurrection who was released in the place of Jesus, was a Zealot.

The well-known Pharisee, Gamaliel, spoke of the early history of Judah and this movement, when he was addressing the high priests and members of the Sadducees about the uproar caused in opposition to Peter and the other apostles. He told them, "*Judas the Galilean appeared in the days of the census and led a band of people in revolt. He too was killed, and all his followers were scattered*"

(Acts 5:37). He was probably killed by Herod Antipas, who also murdered John the Baptist (Matthew 14:1-12).

The Zealots were ruthless, hunted by the Romans and killed, but their zeal was so great that they did not fear what the Romans could do to them. They may have carried a knife, just in case a Roman came across their path. Historians blame the Zealots for bringing about the final destruction of the Jewish state. The Zealots did not destroy Rome but they destroyed their own nation. In AD 70, the Romans surrounded Jerusalem for a final showdown with the Jews, when the people were starving and in a hopeless situation. The Zealots were so crazed with hate for Rome that they began to murder anyone who was prepared to befriend and accept the Romans. Surrender was a betrayal of God and country they said, and so they started a civil war within the city.

When the Romans took the city, the Zealots were the last to perish. They were in Masada, the last stronghold. When escape was seen to be impossible, Eleazer told his men to slaughter their wives and children and then commit suicide, which they did, and 960 people perished. Only two women and five children escaped by hiding. So the Zealots perished by their own hands, illustrating the self-destructive nature of fanaticism.

It is thought by some that Simon was a member of the very fierce and fanatical political sect of the Jews called the Zealots and these facts help us understand his background. We have no record of how much he personally was involved, although he must have been involved in some way because the nickname they gave him stuck for life – "Simon the Zealot."

Simon the Zealot becomes a disciple

Scripture does not tell us the circumstance that led to Simon becoming a disciple. We do not know if Simon saw in Jesus a reformer who was also opposed to Roman rule and would restore the kingdom to Israel. Perhaps he misinterpreted the motive behind Jesus speaking out against evil in the society and His condemnation of the hypocritical Pharisees. Perhaps he saw Jesus cleansing the temple and liked His zeal when He "*made a whip of cords, and drove all from the temple area ... To those who sold doves he said, 'Get these out of here! How dare you turn my Father's house into a market*'" (John 2:15-16).

Simon the Zealot became Simon the apostle. We might wonder why Jesus should choose such a man and why scripture records nothing of him but his name. The irony increases when we add the fact that Matthew was a tax collector. Tax collectors were very much in league with Rome. There were probably no two groups of Jews in Palestine who hated each other more than the tax collectors and the Zealots. Yet, Jesus chose one of each. Most people probably would have been afraid that these two men would kill each other, but the Lord was not. He knew the kingdom of God was more powerful than the hatred of men. The very fact Jesus chose two men so opposite in their world views, was a demonstration of its power.

The choosing of such men just goes to show the depth of change which Jesus can bring about in a person's life and takes us back to the heart of Jesus, and the heart of the Gospel. Luke 6:12-13 tells us that before Jesus decided who was going to be His disciples, He went out to a mountain and spent the night praying to God. When morning came, He called His disciples and chose twelve, whom He also designated apostles.

Jesus did not randomly choose the disciples. He brought this important issue before His Father in prayer. The appointing did not just happen by accident. Out of many who were following Jesus at the time, these were the ones who would come on the journey of discipleship. Each disciple was divinely appointed and this included Simon the Zealot.

The Zeal of Simon the Zealot

Simon never ceased to be known as 'Simon the Zealot.' Perhaps this was because he never lost his zeal, although it was directed another way through the love of Christ.

Jehu said, "*Come see my zeal for the Lord*" (2 Kings 10:16). He was excited to be doing what he understood was the will of God, and was eager to share his own zeal. After all, enthusiasm is contagious; those infected want others to be involved.

Many people have a passion and zeal for many things whether that be a sport, a hobby or work, and it is good to see zeal, if it is directed in the right way and for the right reason.

What is zeal in religion? It is a burning desire to please God; to do His will, and to advance His glory in the world in every possible way. It is a desire the Holy Spirit puts in the heart of the believer when he or she is converted.

A zealous person in religion is a person who sees, cares and lives for one thing, and that one thing is to please God. Whether that person has health or sickness, is rich or poor; pleases or displeases man, receives honour or shame, for all this the zealous person cares nothing at all.

Just as exercise is good for the health and work is good for the muscles, so zeal is good for our souls. Paul says in Romans 12:11,

"*Never be lacking in zeal, but keep your spiritual fervour, serving the Lord.*" There is no doubt that many professing Christians today who, if they had lived in the days when our Lord and His apostles walked on earth, would have called Him and all His followers, extremists and zealots.

Look at the example of the Apostle Paul and hear what he says to the Ephesian elders on his last visit: "*I consider my life worth nothing to me, if only I may finish the race and complete the task the Lord Jesus has given me – the task of testifying to the gospel of God's grace*" (Acts 20:24).

The early Christians witnessed with such enthusiasm that they were called those who "*have caused trouble all over the world*" (Acts 17:6). Simon the Zealot was the type who could get all excited about Jesus. Nothing so much keeps alive true religion as zealous Christians scattered here and there throughout the world.

Why did Jesus invite Simon the Zealot to be an Apostle?

Perhaps Jesus saw the potential for good in Simon. Jesus chose Simon, not for what he was or had been, but for what Simon could become. Isn't this, after all, the same reason Jesus extends His invitation to us?

Jesus accepted each disciple for what he was, and if their background and viewpoint was of a controversial nature, it made no difference to Him. When He chose Matthew, He was in danger of making the Jewish establishment angry, and when He chose Simon, He was in danger of enraging the Roman authorities.

We are not told what exactly happened that persuaded Simon to become a follower of Jesus. He may have thought Jesus was heading up another revolutionary cause when he heard Jesus talk about a kingdom and seeing the commotion His messages and methods were causing. It turned out that rather than Jesus doing what Simon perhaps expected, Jesus changed him.

Obviously Simon dramatically changed his approach to life since Jesus taught His followers to be peaceful in their relationship with the Roman government. In terms of taxes, He encouraged everyone to *"Give to Caesar what is Caesar's, and to God what is God's"* (Matthew 22:21). He taught His disciples to *"Love your enemies and pray for those who persecute you"* (Matthew 5:44). Simon had been a man of violence who became a man of peace and even though the Zealots and Publicans were bitter enemies, Jesus chose a disciple from both groups and they worked together for the kingdom of God. Here were two men, Matthew and Simon, with completely opposite perspectives, working side by side for the kingdom of God. That is what can happen when Jesus Christ enters and changes a life.

Simon the Zealot's final days

The last reference we have of Simon the Zealot in scripture is in Acts 1:13, where he was one of the company present with the other disciples in the Upper Room at Pentecost.

Many legends surround what happened after that and of his missionary journeys. The early Christians must have travelled far and wide or else Christianity could not have spread so quickly throughout the Roman Empire. We remember that on the day of Pentecost, people from the entire Mediterranean world were visiting Jerusalem. Of the three thousand converted, many must have returned to their own country and spread the gospel message.

Due to the vast network of Roman roads all over the empire, travel in the first century was made comparatively easy. Not only did the Romans force local people in each area to build the roads but the Romans themselves also built and protected them.

Several sources say that Simon left Jerusalem and travelled to Egypt and then through North Africa to Carthage. In Greek and Roman times, Carthage was seen as the capital of a much larger empire called "Libya." From there, Simon travelled to Spain and north to Britain.

Dorotheus, Bishop of Tyre, wrote around AD 300, that Simon preached in Mauretania, one of the countries of North Africa and in Britain. Nicephorus of Constantinople (AD 758-828) maintained that Simon preached in Egypt, Africa, Libya, Mauretania and finally in Britain. The Coptic Church in North Africa has a tradition that Simon travelled in Egypt, Africa and Britain and that he was martyred in Iran.

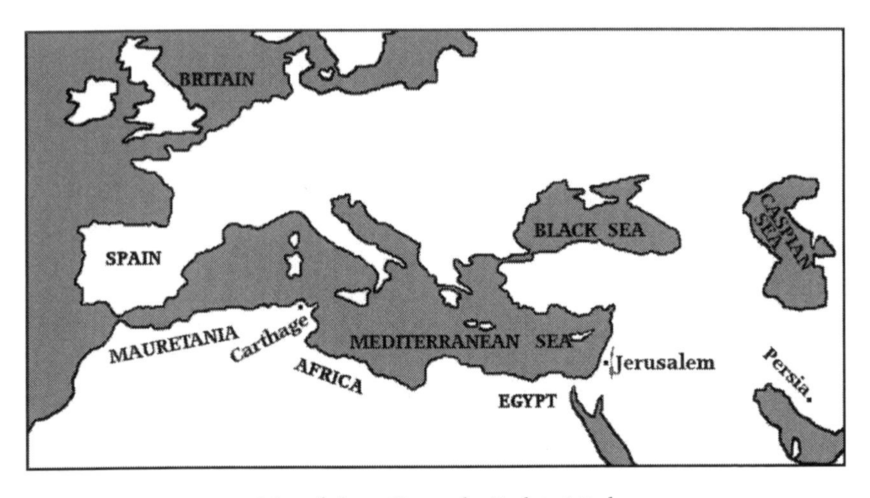

Map of places Simon the Zealot visited

If these accounts are accurate Simon must have begun his work among the large number of Jews in Egypt, and then slowly moved westward into Libya and then Mauretania.

There is no evidence that any churches were founded in Britain by Simon, perhaps he was only there a very short time. Simon would probably have ministered to people with whom he could communicate. This would be the Greek and Latin speaking Roman troops and their families. Probably some Britons could speak Latin due to their commercial relations with the Romans, and it is possible that Britons visited Rome to do trade and were converted and took the gospel back to Britain.

We are not sure when Christianity came to Britain but the African, Tertullian, writing about AD 200, spoke of 'the land of the Britons, not reached by Rome but subject to Christ,' implying that Christianity was introduced there before Roman rule. He also referred to Britain as a land 'where Christ's name reigns.'

There is a strong tradition that Simon was in Persia with the apostle Jude where they worked together. It is widely believed that both Simon and Jude were martyred together in Persia in AD 65. Some historians claim he was crucified and others say he was sawn in two. Some artists show a picture of Simon with a saw, the instrument of his death, while others show him with a book, symbolic of his zeal for the Law.

Final comment

Simon was a Jewish Zealot who wanted to set his people free from Roman oppression and perhaps thought Jesus would be the one to initiate that. He saw Jesus crucified on the cross and then after His resurrection, he became a zealot of the Gospel.

Let us not forget that after Christ chose Simon as an apostle, he did not cease to be known as 'the Zealot.' Although scripture does not record anything that he was involved in or said, Jesus chose him for a reason and only eternity will reveal how God's plan was realised.

Today there are many followers of Christ who are quietly labouring for their Master and comparatively little is known about them, nor do they get the praise of men, but one day they will receive their reward. Let us therefore be encouraged to remain faithful wherever God has placed us in these days.

Paul says in Romans 12:11, "*Never be lacking in zeal, but keep your spiritual fervour, serving the Lord.*" Are you lacking in zeal? Zeal is good for the soul. It is good for the church and it is good for the world. Ask God to give you zeal for His work; to win souls for Christ; to tell the world that the Saviour has come. Jesus chose a Zealot to be one of His disciples - will we also be zealous for Him?

Judas Iscariot
who betrayed Jesus

The first reference to Judas Iscariot is when he is listed as one of the disciples (Matt.10:4; Mark 3:19; Luke 6:16). The call of Judas is not recorded in scripture and we are not told when and how he became a disciple of Jesus.

The fact the New Testament affirms that Jesus personally chose Judas Iscariot, indicates he possessed the same potential as the other disciples. Jesus had spent a night in prayer before choosing the Twelve, and Judas Iscariot was among those chosen (Luke 6:12-16).

Judas was once a proud name, a form of Judah, which means "praised." The fourth son of the patriarch Jacob and his wife Leah was called Judah, who became the father of the Israelite tribe of Judah. Jesus had a brother named Judas (Matt. 13:55), who probably wrote the Epistle of Jude. There was also another of the Twelve called Judas but he was clearly distinguished from the traitor (John 14:22).

The origin of the surname Iscariot is uncertain. According to one theory, the name means "man of Kerioth," and refers to a town or area in ancient Judea. If correct, this would suggest that

Judas came from southern Palestine, whereas the other disciples were probably Galileans from the north. Another theory is that a copyist's error transposed two letters and that Judas was named "Sicariot," a member of the party of the Sicarii. This comes from the Greek word for "assassins" and is a reference to a group of fanatical nationalists who thought that the only good Roman was a dead Roman. Judas might have originally been a member of this group.

To all appearances, at least, at the beginning, Judas was a most eligible person to be a chosen disciple, a man of promise with high ideals. There is no record that he had a dishonourable past like the tax collector, Matthew Levi. Also, Simon Peter was famous for his impulsiveness and James and John for their temper, nothing uncomplimentary is mentioned about Judas' character.

Judas was called to follow Christ, called to be an apostle, called to be one of those who were to lay the foundation of the church. Judas was someone with great promise in life but made his own choice to be a traitor. Perhaps as a Judean, he did not have a close bond with the other disciples. This could have made him more vulnerable to disloyalty, and could have explained his affinity with the scribes and Pharisees. His father's name was Simon Iscariot who appeared to be known to John (John 6:71; 13:2). This Simon is unknown to us.

Like the other eleven, Judas must have left whatever employment he may have been involved in and began to follow Jesus full-time. He began exactly like the others with no special gifts and without any characteristics that made him stand out from the group.

For three years he was with the Lord and the other disciples. He walked and talked with the Son of God. He heard the most wonderful preaching from the lips of Jesus, he watched as amazing miracles were performed, he broke bread with Him, he even stayed with Jesus when less committed disciples began to leave the group (John 6:66-71). He had devoted his life to following Jesus.

Judas was sincere in his initial discipleship, having an honest desire to follow Jesus. In fact he was so highly respected by the other disciples that he was appointed the treasurer. The choice of Judas as treasurer of the Twelve showed that his companions had confidence in him. Though Matthew, as a tax collector, would have plenty of experience with money, Judas must have shown some evidence of financial ability. Also, he won their respect as trustworthy and responsible. As a result, he was given the task of looking after the bag into which went all gifts, and from which came all expenses. He never gave the slightest hint that he would eventually steal from those funds (John 12:6).

Jesus said, "One of you is a Devil"
(John 6:70-71)

After Jesus performed the miracle of feeding the five thousand people with a boy's lunch of five small barley loves and two small fish, He explained He was the bread of life. He said, "*I am the bread of life. He who comes to me will never go hungry, and he who believes in me will never be thirsty*" (John 6:35). Jesus then went on to explain in greater detail what He meant (John 6:41-59). On hearing this, the majority of people could not understand what Jesus was saying and many turned back and no longer followed Him (John 6:60-66). Then Jesus asked his disciples a pointed question, "*You do not want to leave too, do you?*" (John 6:67).

In response to the question, Peter made a great confession of faith when he said, "*Lord to whom shall we go? You have the words of eternal life. We believe and know that you are the Holy One of God*" (John 6:68-69).

Clearly Peter was saying that Jesus is the only one who can satisfy the desires of the soul, there is no one else to turn to. Peter was declaring that Jesus' words were not empty statements, they were life changing words. Jesus said, "*The words I have spoken to you are spirit and they are life*" (John 6:63). How true that is, no one but Jesus can give us the knowledge of God. He alone has the words of eternal life.

Peter had spoken on behalf of the Twelve, saying, "*We believe and know ....*" Yet there was one person present who did not have the same convictions as Peter. As Jesus looked upon His group of twelve men, He knew that there was one exception. Peter made a mistake for he was sure that all the apostles were believers, which shows how convincing Judas was.

When Jesus should have drawn comfort from Peter's words and commended the Twelve for sticking with Him, He made another staggering statement, "*Have I not chosen you, the Twelve? Yet one of you is a devil!*" (v.70). The Greek word '*diabolos*' means slanderer, false accuser. This one man was under the control of the devil.

Obviously, the other eleven disciples had no idea that Judas was not one of them in that he was not a true believer. This reminds us how true is the saying, "*Man looks at the outward appearance but God looks at the heart*" (1 Samuel 16:7).

All twelve had equally been given tremendous privileges and opportunities and yet one of them had never opened his heart to the Saviour. Judas was one of those who kept company with Jesus for His entire ministry and yet he will be separated from Jesus for eternity.

Jesus did not say at this stage that Judas would betray Him or how he would do it. It is the writer himself who writes this word of explanation in verse 71. Jesus was sending a message to

Judas, letting him know that one day he would betray Him. There was also the challenge to all of His disciples to guard their hearts against Satan's schemes.

Those words and actions of Jesus can also encourage church and ministry leaders to continue leading, even though there is a possibility that some of the people they serve could hurt or leave the fellowship. Although it is natural for Pastors and Christian leaders to hope that people would not leave their congregations or ministries, they should not let that concern become a source of constant worry or anxiety that consequently could hinder their work.

Jesus did not let the fear of what Judas was going to do cause Him to withdraw from the Twelve. On the contrary, John 13:1 says: *"Having loved His own who were in the world, he now showed them the full extent of his love."* Jesus didn't take it personally when many of His disciples turned back and no longer followed Him.

A wise leader recognises that there will always be people who will struggle to follow the teaching they may be given. Jesus only lost one of the Twelve. It is true that the pain of betrayal or rejection can bring discouragement and loss of joy to those in leadership, but it is helpful to remember that, even though Judas betrayed Jesus, His closest followers remained faithful to Him. When Pastors and Christian leaders evaluate their ministries, they will possibly discover that their success rate will also greatly exceed their rejection rate.

Judas wanted money to give to the poor

(Matthew 26:6-13; Mark 14:3-9; John 12:3-8)

Six days before Jesus would celebrate the last Passover on this earth, He came to Bethany. Matthew and Mark tell us that He was in the home of a man called Simon the leper (Matthew 26:6-13; Mark 14:3-9; John 12:3-8). John reminds us that it was in Bethany where Jesus raised Lazarus from the dead.

A dinner was being held, probably in gratitude for Jesus raising Lazarus from the dead and perhaps also for the healing of Simon, who had been a leper, and was still called 'Simon the leper.' Hence the dinner was in the home of Simon the leper, with Lazarus also present. Lazarus' sister Martha helped to serve the meal.

While the guests were reclining at the table, the other sister Mary took an alabaster jar of very expensive perfume and poured it on Jesus head. Matthew and Mark record that she anointed Jesus head while John records that she anointed and wiped His feet with her hair. When we examine the whole picture she must have anointed both His head and His feet, or the ointment had dripped onto His feet – each writer recorded the event as he saw it happen.

Matthew and Mark tell us that when those present saw this they were indignant and asked, "*Why this waste?*" But John tells us that Judas Iscariot objected, "*Why wasn't this perfume sold and the money given to the poor?*"

Mary's heart was flowing with love and gratitude to Jesus for what He had done for her brother Lazarus but, in contrast, Judas Iscariot was critical of what she was doing.

Judas estimated that the jar of perfume was worth the equivalent of what a labourer would receive for three hundred days of work. Judas obviously had money on his mind and scripture reminds us that "*the love of money is a root of all kinds of evil*" (1 Timothy 6:10).

With the benefit of writing his Gospel years after the event, John was able to add, "*He did not say this because he cared about the poor but because he was a thief*" (John 12:6). Here, John is revealing the true character of Judas, and why he wanted the monetary equivalent of the perfume to be entrusted to him. He was pretending to show zeal and concern for the poor and speaking as if his concern for the poor exceeded that of the other disciples. Sadly, however, he was not motivated by love for the poor but by personal greed.

Judas, as the treasurer, had the confidence of the other disciples. No one was checking his accounts at this point and he had the opportunity to exploit their trust. John gave his assessment of the heart of Judas Iscariot, branding him a thief, after the truth about Judas Iscariot became apparent to his fellow disciples.

In response to Judas Iscariot's unwarranted and self-motivated criticism, Jesus was quick to defend Mary and rebuked Judas … "*Leave her alone, it was meant that she should save this perfume for the day of my burial*" (John 12:7). Jesus knew the love and devotion of Mary in contrast to the selfishness and deceit of Judas. This was an act of love from Mary prompted by the fact that Jesus had raised her brother from the dead and her understanding that Jesus was about to die. She understood the sorrow Jesus was going through and wanted to identify with Him in His sorrow.

Jesus was heading for Jerusalem and death. Mary had, in fact, anticipated His burial, "*She did what she could. She poured perfume on my body beforehand to prepare for my burial*" (Mark 14:8). While she may not have understood it that way, Jesus applied deep meaning to her action. For Mary, her act was simply a way of showing her Lord how much she loved Him. However, from God's point of view, her act marked the start of our Lord's Passion, consisting of His terrible sufferings from His agony in the garden, and coming to a climax in His death upon the cross.

This is why Jesus said, "*You will always have the poor among you, but you will not always have me*" (John 12:8). If Mary had not anointed the Lord with the perfume at that time, she would not have had another opportunity to do so. Jesus was on His way to the cross and they failed to see the priority of the hour. They could help the poor at any time, but Jesus would not be with them in the flesh much longer.

Mary gave her most precious possession to prepare Jesus for burial. She was listening to Jesus' words and she heard the pain in His voice as He told them He was going to be killed. She had learned from Jesus about the resurrection, and about the good news of another kingdom that was coming which would never pass away.

She poured some perfume on his head, anointing him like a king. Then she stooped down and poured some on his feet, going even beyond what a servant might do as she wiped his feet with her own hair. Mary's humble, loving service was to prepare Jesus for his burial. It was a timely gift as it would be six days later that Jesus' body would be beaten and bruised.

Jesus confirmed that what she had done would form part of the gospel story and would be told over and over again and this, in fact, has happened to this day. *"I tell you the truth, wherever the gospel is preached throughout the world, what she has done will also be told, in memory of her"* (Mark 14:9).

The apostle Paul wrote, "*Christ loved us and gave himself up for us as a fragrant offering and sacrifice to God*" (Ephesians 5:2). As loving as Mary's offering was, Christ loved us enough to suffer our punishment and die in our stead. Christ's offering was the greatest offering of all—a fragrant offering and sacrifice to God.

On the other hand, Judas was not concerned with the glory of God; he was consumed with self, which was the opposite of Jesus' teachings and of what Mary was doing, so he never knew the truth that would set him free.

Jesus Predicted Judas Would Betray Him

(Matthew 26:20-25; Mark 14:17-21; John 13:18-30)

According to John's Gospel, Jesus had already given His disciples a lesson in humility when He washed their feet. Afterwards He amazed them by saying that one of them was going to betray Him. This was a shock to them – it would not be an enemy – but one of His chosen Twelve would betray Him. One can only imagine how surprised they would have been. What did their Master mean by saying that one of them would betray Him?

According to Matthew, this happened while they were eating the Passover meal and, in disbelief, they began to question Jesus one after the other, with the exception of Judas Iscariot, *"Surely not I, Lord."* In reply Jesus said, *"The one who has dipped his hand into the bowl with me will betray me"* (Matthew 26:23).

By saying this, Jesus was making the betrayal appear even more horrific. Someone who had dipped his hand into the dish and shared in communion with Jesus would betray Him. To treat a host in such a manner was unthinkable. By Jesus making this statement, He was exposing the great wickedness of Judas's crime and sought to stir his conscience about his evil deed and perhaps he would repent at the last moment. Jesus was revealing to Judas that He already knew what he was about to do.

Jesus still did not make it clear which of the Twelve would betray Him as all of them would have dipped their hand in the bowl with Him. Then Judas said, *"Surely not I, Rabbi?"* Perhaps he said this to divert attention from himself and also avoid suspicion by his silence of what he was about to do. Therefore, he followed the others in asking the same question.

It is notable that Judas did not follow the others and substituted

'Rabbi' for 'Lord'. Others said, "*Surely not I, Lord*," but Judas could only say "*Surely not I, Rabbi*." Lord meant one with authority over you and Rabbi was your teacher. A teacher would have great influence in your life, but not the authority that the Lord would have. Was Judas conscious that Jesus was not his Lord?

Here we see a tremendous act of God's compassion reaching out to Judas. Even while Judas was planning to betray Him, Jesus still reached out to him, trying to change his heart and life. But the disciples themselves could not see any fault in Judas.

What possible motive or motives would Judas have that would lead him to betray Jesus Christ? We must understand that Judas did not do this because he was set apart or chosen by God for this wicked deed. Scripture does record that it had been prophesied hundreds of years earlier that a close friend would voluntarily betray the Messiah for thirty pieces of silver (Ps. 41:9, 109:5-8, Zechariah 11:12-13).

Jesus himself said, "*The Son of Man will go as it has been decreed, but woe to that man who betrays him*" (Luke 22:22). However, the fact this betrayal was predicted does not absolve Judas Iscariot of guilt.

Clearly Judas was fully responsible and accountable for his actions. Judas had a free choice and took the step voluntarily to betray Jesus to the enemy. He persevered in his plan despite the many warnings given by Jesus. The Lord had warned ... "*The Son of man will go just as it is written about him. But woe to that man who betrays the Son of Man! It would be better for him if he had not been born*" (Matthew. 26:24).

Judas Iscariot had just as much potential of becoming what the eleven other apostles became as he had of becoming a traitor. Judas was not a pawn in a pre-determined plan that he had no power to resist. He chose to act as he did and became a tool of Satan.

Judas Made Arrangements to Betray Jesus

(Matthew 26:14-16; Mark 14:10-11; Luke 22:3-6)

In contrast from an expression of Mary's love and devotion, Matthew records the most deadly deed of disloyalty. Judas Iscariot, one of Jesus' chosen Twelve, had gone to the chief priests to discuss terms about betraying Jesus to them.

The chief priests and elders had previously met to discuss how they would "*arrest Jesus in some sly way and kill him*" (Matthew 26:4). They were looking for a quiet way to arrest Jesus without His supporters creating a riot. However, they did not come to a conclusion how they could do that.

Then, without prior notice, Judas Iscariot, one of Jesus' close friends, went to the chief priests and offered to help them. Judas asked, "*What are you willing to give me if I hand him over to you?*" (Matthew 26:15).

The chief priests and elders did not send for Judas or make the proposal to him. They were not to have known that one of Christ's disciples could be tempted or even consider betraying their Master. They were delighted that Judas had come to them and immediately decided to give him money. He agreed to receive thirty pieces of silver - the exact amount prophesied centuries before, "*So they paid me thirty pieces of silver*" (Zechariah 11:12). The thirty pieces of silver was also the cost of a common slave at that time and was another way of humiliating Jesus (Exodus 21:32).

After the agreement was made, Judas looked for an opportunity to betray Jesus.

Here we see that Judas personally, willingly and of his own initiative, decided to betray Jesus. If he had disagreed with something Jesus said or did, he could have simply walked away. This is what others had done. John tells us how some disciples found Jesus' teaching hard to take (John 6:60) and decided to leave Him. "*From this time many of his disciples turned back and no longer followed him*" (John 6:66). Judas on the other hand, remained with Jesus as one of the twelve chosen disciples.

Here was a man who had the highest privileges possible. He was chosen by the Lord Himself to be a disciple and had witnessed our Lord's miracles and heard His teaching. Judas heard the Sermon on the Mount, and also the lessons taught from the parables. He saw the blind receive their sight, the deaf their hearing, and the dead raised to life. He witnessed Jesus still the storm, cast out demons, cast the money changers out of the temple, and taking little children in His arms to bless them. He was a companion of Peter, James and John. With the other apostles, Judas would have gone on preaching missions for the Lord and cast out demons (Luke 10:17-20). Judas received the same privileges as the rest of the Twelve. From every viewpoint, Judas was so like the other disciples that they did not suspect any flaw in his character or that he was a thief or disloyal to their Master.

There is only one thing that can account for Judas doing such a wicked thing to his Master – the love of money. Judas asked the chief priests, "*What are you willing to give me?*" Judas was willing to betray Jesus for money.

Surely Judas did not lack anything. Like the other disciples, he would have been well provided for when he was with Jesus. In fact, at this time, they had just had a meal in the house of Simon the leper. Jesus had said earlier to His disciples, "*Watch out! Be on your guard against all kinds of greed; a man's life does not consist in the abundance of his possessions*" (Luke 12:15).

Judas had not learnt the lesson and the danger of greed in his own life. Scripture is full of proof of how Satan can corrupt and spoil men and women's lives:

In the Garden of Eden, Eve coveted the forbidden fruit and brought sin and death into the world (Genesis 3:1-24).

At Ai, Achan coveted some gold, silver and expensive garments and brought defeat to a nation and death to himself and his family (Joshua 7:1-26).

David coveted Bathsheba, Uriah's wife, and as a result brought the sword of God into his household for generations (2 Samuel 11:1 -12:10).

Ahab coveted Naboth's vineyard and committed murder in his attempt to grab what belonged to another (1 Kings 21:1-16).

When Gehazi, the servant of Elisha, saw that Elisha refused Naaman's treasures after he was healed of leprosy, he coveted them and became leprous as punishment (2 Kings 5:20-27).

Ananias and Sapphira lied to the Holy Spirit because they coveted money they received from the sale of land and were punished by death (Acts 5:1-11).

If the love of money is what led Judas to betray Jesus, then it would tell us that the love of money has the ability to cause us to go astray. If we are willing to compromise moral and spiritual principles for money or other worldly gains, then they are too important in our lives.

The writer to the Hebrews reminds us to "*Keep your life free from the love of money, and be content with what you have, for God has said, 'Never will I leave you; never will I forsake you'*" (Hebrews 13:5). The apostle Paul told Timothy, "*People who want to get rich fall into temptation*" (1Timothy 6:9).

For Jesus to be betrayed by a close friend, and one of the Twelve, was much more painful than to be betrayed by any other person. The Psalmist said, *"If an enemy were insulting me, I could endure it; if a foe were raising himself against me, I could hide from him. But it is you, a man like myself, my companion, my close friend, with whom I enjoyed sweet fellowship"* (Psalm 55: 12-14).

Judas looked for an opportunity to betray Jesus to the chief priests when He would be away from the crowd. However, Judas did not seem to understand that nothing is done in secret and Jesus knew all about what he was going to do.

Why did Judas do this? We are told "*Then Satan entered Judas, called Iscariot, one of the Twelve*" (Luke 22:3). It is clear that Satan took an active part in Judas' betrayal of Jesus, but this does not exclude Judas from personal blame. Judas was guilty because he did not resist the devil. Peter tells us, "*Resist him, standing firm in the faith*" (1 Peter 5:9).

"*Woe to that man by whom the Son of Man is betrayed*" reveals the guilt and the doom of the traitor. Not to have been born would have been better for such a man. But he was born, and was in the process of committing the dreadful deed. What makes his shame all the more horrible is the fact that he not only planned the betrayal, but of his own free will took the next step – volunteering to deliver Jesus to the enemy and accepting the thirty pieces of silver! In spite of Christ's remarkable warnings, Judas continued with what he had planned.

When we compare Zechariah 11:12-13 with Matthew 27:9-10, we see that another prophecy about Judas was fulfilled. In describing the betrayal, all three Synoptic gospels point out that he was *"one of the Twelve"* (Matt. 26:47; Mark 14:10, 43, Luke 22:3, 47). The fact that the betrayer came from among the Lord's closest friends cannot be overlooked.

There are many today who associate with Christians and take an active part in religious services but have never known Christ themselves.

Judas knew what he was going to do and yet was willing to reach out and take the bread that Jesus offered him. This was the final act of treachery, there was no turning back. Now it was all over with Judas and there was no more possibility of repentance. So Judas went out into the night and informed the authorities where Jesus could be found.

Judas Betrayed Jesus with a Kiss

(Matthew 26:47-50; Mark 14:43-46; Luke 22:47-54a; John 18:2-13)

Matthew tells us that when Jesus and His disciples had finished celebrating the Passover (the Lord's Supper) with the singing of a hymn, they went out to the Mount of Olives. At the Mount of Olives was a grove called Gethsemane. It probably was an area surrounded by olive trees to make it private. As Jesus visited this spot frequently with His disciples, it may have been owned by one of His followers (John 18:2).

Jesus left eight of His disciples near the entrance to the grove while He took Peter, James and John with Him into it. There, Jesus revealed to His three close friends how troubled and sorrowful He was. He said to them, *"My soul is overwhelmed with sorrow to the point of death. Stay here and keep watch with me."* Jesus went further into the grove and agonised in prayer. When He returned He found His three friends sleeping. He informed them that the time had come for Him to be betrayed into the hands of the enemies. "*Rise, let us go! Here comes my betrayer!*" (Matthew 26:46).

Jesus had just exposed Judas for what he was about to do and said to him, "*What you are about to do, do quickly*" (John 13:27). The other disciples did not understand why Jesus was saying this to Judas. Perhaps they thought Jesus had asked Judas, as treasurer, to do something quickly.

Events started to move very fast. It is quite possible that Judas was afraid that what he had planned to do would become known by the other disciples and they could prevent him from carrying out his plans.

After the Passover meal, Judas had gone back to the chief priests and elders to inform them that he would take them to Jesus, where they could arrest Him with no crowd around. We are told, "*a large crowd armed with swords and clubs*" came to arrest Jesus (Matthew 26:47). Did they expect His disciples to put up a fight? They obviously did not understand that Jesus was a man of peace and as a result He offered no resistance.

Perhaps the chief priests were waiting for Judas to come back to them to tell them where they could arrest Jesus. Apparently, they were able to gather up a crowd very quickly and followed Judas to apprehend Jesus. Remember, this was not a sudden impulse for Judas. This evil act had been carefully planned for some time. He had already taken the money for it (Matthew 26:14-16). He had just been waiting for the best opportunity to betray Jesus. In the mean time, he had kept up the pretence that he was fully committed to Christ like the other apostles.

The arresting party, which accompanied Judas, consisted of the officers and men from the temple guard or Levitical police, Pharisees, scribes, servants, chief priests, captains of the temple and elders. They were well supplied with lights, for while the Passover is always held when the moon is full, the moon at this time of night would be near setting, and the valley of the Kidron, in which Gethsemane lay, would be darkened by the olive trees and also the shadow of the adjoining mountain.

Therefore, to prevent the possibility of error, Judas had arranged a signal that would identify Jesus to the soldiers, so the arrest could be made quickly and quietly. He chose a practical signal. In those days, disciples normally greeted their teacher by placing their hands on the rabbi's shoulders and kissing him.

Judas could have so easily stood in the background and pointed out to the soldiers who Jesus was, but he carried out his hypocrisy and evil deed to the very end by going up to Jesus, looking Him in the eyes and kissing Him. Judas betrayed the perfect, sinless, holy Son of God for a few silver coins. "*Then the men stepped forward, seized Jesus and arrested him*" (Matthew 26:50).

We do not know all that contributed to the action Judas took. It could have been that jealousy was part of it. It may have been that greed contributed to Judas' motive. Some people believe that Judas was trying to force Jesus to use His powers to set up an earthly kingdom. He was trying to trick Jesus into leading a revolt against Roman rule.

How do we reconcile the fact that Judas acted out of his own free will, and yet his betrayal of Jesus was prophesied and predetermined in scripture many centuries earlier? Since scripture says that Jesus knew from the beginning who would betray Him (John 6:64) we might wonder if Judas Iscariot can be condemned for his actions. Nevertheless, despite the apparent tension, these two facts are not in conflict and do not need to be reconciled. God did not decree in advance, or compel Judas, or set him up for this assignment. Jesus did not call Judas to be a disciple so that he would fill the function of the betrayer. If He did, then Jesus encouraged Judas to sin and our Lord does not do that. As James 1:13 says, "*God cannot be tempted by evil, nor does he tempt anyone.*"

No outside influence forced Judas to betray Christ. He was responsible for his own actions. God's plan and Judas' act of betrayal agree perfectly. Judas did what he did because his heart was evil. God had foreordained that Jesus would be betrayed and that He would die for the sins of the world. Jesus Himself affirmed both truths when He said, "*The Son of Man will go just as it is written about him. But woe to that man who betrays the Son of Man! It would be better for him if he had not been born*" (Matthew 26:24). Scripture reminds us that God "*works out everything in conformity with the purpose of his will*" (Ephesians 1:11).

The method by which Christ would die was planned by God, and yet by his own choice, Judas carried out his evil deed without any external force - both incidents are true. The perfect will of God and the wicked desire of Judas combined to bring about Christ's death. Judas did it for evil, but God meant it for good and there is no contradiction.

When Joseph was sold into Egypt by his brothers he said, "*You intended to harm me, but God intended it for good to accomplish what is now being done, the saving of many lives*" (Genesis 50:20). Similarly, Judas meant harm by betraying Jesus but God used the betrayal for the salvation of mankind.

When Jesus called Judas, he had the same potential as the other disciples, but he did not surrender his life to Jesus as the others had done. His heart had never been changed and he became the one to betray Jesus into the hands of His enemies.

Judas' Tragic death

(Matthew 27:3-5; Acts 1:18-19)

As the Romans took Jesus away, Judas saw that his awful deed had gone disastrously wrong. Matthew tells us that when Judas saw Jesus had been condemned "*he was seized with remorse and returned the thirty silver coins to the chief priests and elders. 'I have sinned,' he said, 'for I have betrayed innocent blood'"* (Matthew 27:3-4). The money, which had been so important to him before, was something he no longer wanted.

Judas had been planning his evil deed for some time but as soon as it happened he was filled with remorse for what he had done. His remorse was not the same as repentance. There is no indication that he was prepared to confess his sin and ask the Saviour's forgiveness. He was sorry, not because he had sinned, but that things did not work out as he had planned. He received no sympathy from the chief priests and elders to whom he returned to confess what he had done was wrong, and gave back the money he had received from them. They simply told him, "*What is that to us? That's your responsibility*" (Matthew 27:4). They had received what they wanted (the arrest of Jesus) and had no longer an interest in Judas or his "blood money."

Putting the two accounts of Judas' death together, we get a fuller description of what happened. Both events are true, but they did not happen at the same time. Matthew tells us that Judas died by hanging (Matthew 27:3-8). Luke tells us that he fell headlong and his bowels gushed out (Acts 1:18-19). As a result of these differing accounts, some critics claim a contradiction in the two accounts of his death given by Matthew and Luke (the author of Acts).

However, there is no contradiction here because both are true. A contradiction occurs when one statement eliminates the possibility of another. It is not a contradiction to describe an event in two different ways. Therefore, it is possible to say that Judas hanged himself and Judas fell down. Both are possible since neither denies the possibility of the other.

The standard explanation given is that Judas hanged himself on a tree at the edge of a cliff and then his body fell on the rocks below and burst open. Judas hanged himself on Passover and before the

Sabbath, and no Jew was going to touch the hanging corpse. Also, touching a dead body caused defilement (Numbers 9:6; Numbers 19:13; Haggai 2:13) and it would have been considered work to take it down on the Sabbath. Horrible as it is, Judas' dead body hung in the hot sun of Jerusalem and became swollen as a result of the build up of gases. Judas' body hit the ground (due to the branch he hung on or the rope itself breaking) and burst open with his internal organs spilling out.

Matthew completes his account of Judas by saying that the chief priests took the silver pieces that Judas had thrown into the temple and said, *"It is against the law to put this into the treasury, it is blood money."* After some discussion they decided to buy the potter's field with it, to bury strangers in. Therefore that field has been *"called the Field of Blood to this day"* (Matthew 27:6-8).

However, another account of the purchase of this field is given by Luke in Acts 1:18-19. He tells us *"With the reward he got for his wickedness, Judas bought a field."* It was purchased by the chief priests with the money Judas returned which he had received for betraying Jesus. As the field was bought with Judas' money by proxy, it became his possession. So it is correct to say that "Judas bought a field."

When Jesus was being crucified He said, *"Father, forgive them, for they do not know what they are doing"* (Luke 23:34). A few moments later, the criminal beside Jesus asked Him to *"remember me when you come into your kingdom."* Jesus turned to him and said, *"I tell you the truth, today you will be with me in paradise"* (Luke 23:42-43). Surely, if the criminal on the cross beside Jesus had asked for mercy and received it, then Judas would also have received mercy if he had asked the Saviour for forgiveness.

Just a short time before this, when Jesus was arrested, Peter denied three times that he knew Jesus. However, we are told that

Peter "*went out and wept bitterly*" over the denial of the Master (Luke 22:61-62). After Jesus death and resurrection, Jesus gave Peter a three-fold command to "*feed my sheep*" in John 21:15-17. Each time Jesus said, "*Feed my sheep,*" it was in response to Peter's three-fold declaration of love for Jesus. The setting was one of the last of Jesus' post-resurrection appearances to His disciples on the shores of the Sea of Galilee.

Peter repented and was restored to the Saviour and commissioned to take the Gospel to others. At the commencement of Jesus ministry, He did say, "*Whoever comes to me I will never drive away*" (John 6:37). The story of Judas could have turned out very differently. Instead of ending it all by taking his own life, he could have followed the crowd out to the city gates, gone to the place where the three crosses stood and, like the thief on the cross, asked for mercy and forgiveness. Judas might have become one of the greatest saints for God, because those who are forgiven much, love much. But instead he forfeited his ministry to go to a lost eternity.

Judas had every opportunity to turn from his sin when he was with Jesus for three years. He heard numerous appeals from Christ urging him not to do the deed he was planning to do. He heard every lesson Jesus taught during His ministry. Many of those lessons applied directly to him including the time Jesus told the Twelve, "*One of you is a devil*" (John 6:70), and at the Last Supper saying, "*Woe to the man who betrays the Son of Man*" (Matthew 26:24). Judas listened to all of these warnings and never applied them to himself but kept up his deceit.

The final tragedy of Judas is not what he did, however dreadful. The final tragedy is what he did not do. He could have asked Jesus for forgiveness, and received it. He did not seek the forgiveness of God. He did not cry out for mercy. He did not seek deliverance from Satan. Instead, he tried to silence his conscience by killing himself.

One lesson from Judas' tragedy is that a person's downfall may be concealed from friends and family for a long time, because it starts inside the heart until, one day, it is exposed and the truth is found out. Sin may lie hidden for a long time before it suddenly becomes public knowledge.

Judas Iscariot will be remembered as "*the one who would betray him*" (Matthew 26:25). Judas will go down in history, and as long as the world remains, as the one who sold his Lord for thirty pieces of silver. All else about him is forgotten. Jesus said of the traitor "*It would be better for him if he had not been born*" (Mark 14:21). What an epitaph for a human life!

What a difference it is for the one who surrenders his or her life to the Saviour. Jesus said, "*I am going there to prepare a place for you*" (John 14:1-3). For all who have experienced cleansing and forgiveness from the Saviour, who died on the cross, "*shall not perish but have everlasting life*" (John 3:16).